Praise for TAKE THE LEAD

"The defining difference in this superb book is Myers' insistence that every day provides leadership opportunities for every one of us—from the most junior employee to the top of the organization."

—*The Washington Post*

"A home run. . . . Written in an intelligent but conversational and approachable tone, this inspirational primer is a perfect read for anyone seeking to understand, develop, or unleash his or her genuine leadership potential."

—*Publishers Weekly*

"Myers offers a cogent, articulate addition to modern leadership theory, citing her experiences with both President Clinton and Obama. . . . An enjoyable and insightful read for anyone interested in increasing their personal and professional effectiveness."

—*Kirkus Reviews*

"Betsy Myers, adviser to US presidents and longtime advocate for women, shares her considerable experience and wisdom with everyone who cares about high-level and everyday leadership. This charming, engrossing book will particularly excite and empower women, who will treat this book as their personal mentor and apply Myers's principles to enrich their lives."

—Rosabeth Moss Kanter, Harvard Business School professor and bestselling author of *Confidence* and *SuperCorp*

"A must-read for current and rising leaders. Betsy Myers approaches leadership in a personal, compelling, and actionable way."

—Elliott Masie, chair, The Learning CONSORTIUM

"*Take the Lead* captures essential, practical wisdom, anchored by powerful stories with key insights for any reader who aims to lead."

—Ronald Heifetz, founder of the Center for Public Leadership, John F. Kennedy School of Government, Harvard University

"After forty years of being a boss, I've found *Take the Lead* the most inspirational new tool, not only for leadership but for life."

—Kay Unger, cofounder of Phoebe Couture
and Kay Unger New York

"One of the most topical and well-written business books ever. This book will be given to all leaders in my department, as I believe the concepts Myers discusses are absolutely critical for success in any business."

—Brian Hirshman, senior vice president, Southwest Airlines

"True leadership requires both IQ and EQ—the right combination of head and heart. The leadership principles Betsy Myers illuminates are not only good for business, they are also economic and social imperatives."

—Gloria Cordes Larson, president, Bentley University

"A principled yet practical guide to twenty-first-century leadership. Myers's candid, courageous stories offer convincing evidence of what it takes to be an authentic leader."

—Bill George, author of *True North* and former CEO of Medtronics

"Betsy has a huge heart, tremendous empathy, and a genuine interest in others. That not only makes her a wonderful friend, it also makes her an exceptional leader. In *Take the Lead,* she makes a compelling case that all of us can learn to lead with our hearts."

—Dee Dee Myers, former White House press secretary and *New York Times* bestselling author of *Why Women Should Rule the World*

"In working with some of the most powerful leaders in the world, Betsy has had the opportunity to see into their hearts and minds and understand what makes them inspiring and successful leaders. The result is a book filled with insight and wisdom. "

—Steve Belkin, chairman, Trans National Group

TAKE THE
LEAD

*Motivate, Inspire, and Bring Out the Best
in Yourself and Everyone Around You*

BETSY MYERS
with John David Mann

ATRIA PAPERBACK

NEW YORK · LONDON · TORONTO
SYDNEY · NEW DELHI

To Joanne!
with congrats
and best wishes

Betsy myers
Dec 4, 2018

ATRIA PAPERBACK
A Division of Simon & Schuster, Inc.
1230 Avenue of the Americas
New York, NY 10020

First Atria Paperback edition July 2012

ATRIA PAPERBACK and colophon are trademarks
of Simon & Schuster, Inc.

For information about special discounts for bulk purchases,
please contact Simon & Schuster Special Sales at 1-866-506-1949
or business@simonandschuster.com.

The Simon & Schuster Speakers Bureau can bring authors
to your live event. For more information or to book an event, contact
the Simon & Schuster Speakers Bureau at 1-866-248-3049
or visit our website at www.simonspeakers.com.

Text designed by Paul Dippolito

Manufactured in the United States of America

10   9   8   7   6   5

Library of Congress Cataloging-in-Publication Data

Myers, Betsy.
Take the lead : motivate, inspire, and bring out the best in yourself
and everyone around you / Betsy Myers with John David Mann.
p. cm.
Summary: "Betsy Myers, former executive director of the Center for
Public Leadership at Harvard, Clinton administration insider, and COO
of the Obama campaign, offers 7 key principles for becoming a leader in
every aspect of your life, and the secrets for inspiring and motivating
others toward greater collaboration and action"—Provided by publisher.
Includes index.
1. Leadership—Psychological aspects. 2. Motivation (Psychology).
I. Mann, John David. II. Title.
BF637.L4M94 2011
158'.4—dc22   2011015072

ISBN 978-1-4391-6067-1
ISBN 978-1-4391-6069-5 (pbk)
ISBN 978-1-4391-6395-5 (ebook)

For Madison, my precious daughter,
who teaches me more about love and leadership
than I ever thought possible

CONTENTS

FOREWORD BY DAVID GERGEN

What a delight to welcome to the front ranks of leadership books a fresh, vibrant, down-to-earth voice. Readers of this fine new work will quickly discover here what I began learning a decade ago—that Betsy Myers is special.

I had first heard about Betsy in the early 1990s. She and her sister Dee Dee, the first woman to serve as a US president's press secretary, were rising stars in the Clinton administration. Growing up in California as daughters of a navy pilot, they had each found separate paths into politics. They were both attractive, so they turned heads, but they soon won professional respect because they had good heads of their own. Erskine Bowles, then head of the Small Business Administration and later chief of staff at the White House (yes, the same Erskine who cochaired the national deficit commission in 2010), recognized Betsy's talents and put her in charge of working with women who were small business owners, a growing force in the country. Later Betsy came to the Clinton White House herself to run outreach efforts to women. The president and Hillary often spoke highly of her.

So it was with some curiosity that I greeted her as a student in my classroom at the John F. Kennedy School of Government just as the Clinton years were coming to an end. It was the first year at Harvard for each of us—she in pursuit of a master's degree, me as a rookie on the faculty. What hit me immediately was that she asked thoughtful questions and was one of the best networkers I had ever seen; her warmth and laughter were a magnet for the students who were always buzzing about her.

Neither of us expected to be entwined in each other's lives, but when Betsy agreed after graduation to rescue the alumni relations office at the school and then immediately turned it around, I thought about trying to lure her to the Center for Public Leadership, where I was faculty director. Erskine Bowles confided to me, "Never ask Betsy to do something unless you are sure you want it—because she will always get it done."

It took some wooing on my part, but eventually she agreed to serve as executive director of the center, a decision that proved wonderfully fateful for us both. From my perspective, she was a booster rocket for the center, bringing to it a zest and glamour that inspired the students there. For her, it was a chance not only to build the center but also to make a deep dive into the literature and teachings about leadership. Before long, she was becoming a leadership coach herself.

We were professional partners for three years, working every day to help build a new generation of leaders for America and the world. During those years, Betsy shaped countless lives for the better. You can imagine how mixed my feelings were when she told me one day that a long-shot candidate for the presidency—a freshman senator by the name of Barack Obama—wanted her to become the chief operating officer of his campaign team. Her departure would be a huge loss for the center, but I could also see that it just might be an opportunity of a lifetime for her. And after all, weren't we dedicated to helping new leaders take the stage?

Even though Obama was an underdog, I urged her to take

the job. I had only one caveat: "You know that Hillary is likely to win the nomination," I advised, "and that this may destroy your bridges to her and her husband. But they have been good to you over the years. You have to tell her team—*before* it is announced." She had the courage to do exactly that, and she managed to keep her old friendships intact.

Betsy tells the whole story with verve here in the pages of this book—from her early days as a business entrepreneur through her time with the Clintons, at Harvard, and then on to the Obama team. And you will find packed into these pages valuable lessons about leadership, not only for women—and mothers—but for men as well. Some who write about leadership bring to bear years of experience; others bring an understanding of the literature. Betsy is one of the few who combines both, helping to close the gap between practice and theory.

She is too modest to say so, but Betsy also walks the talk. Over the past couple of decades, she has come to personify some of the most important lessons I have learned about leadership over the years. I might briefly mention three:

First, Betsy illustrates the point that leaders are made, not born.

Yes, some people are born with a little more magic than others. Abe Lincoln attracted a following as a young boy who threw the best wrestlers in town; Dwight Eisenhower was organizing football games when he was a kid, too. But both had long journeys ahead of them before becoming giants of their generations. Lincoln worked for years as an itinerant lawyer and local politician in Illinois before he ascended the national stage, and even then, no one was sure of his capacity to lead. Ike's growth as a leader spurted forward when he was on army assignment to Panama and found a fabulous mentor, General Fox Conner. Even then, though, he remained stuck in the middle ranks of the army, serving sixteen years as a major, before the coming of war allowed him an opportunity to win his stars and become a world-famous leader.

So it was with Betsy. She did not spring forth suddenly as a full-grown leader; she gradually worked her way up, making her share of mistakes and becoming better at each turn in the road. When she first became executive director of the Center for Public Leadership, she found major barriers confronting her. She had to learn how to persuade others to follow her even though they were older and more experienced than she was. She was devoted to expanding opportunities for women, but found that, in some instances, winning the support of a woman as a follower could be more difficult than that of a man. She also had to learn how to bring change in an institution that prided itself on tradition. Surmounting each of these barriers, she became not only a wiser person but a better leader. Indeed, as she and I learned together from our joint mentor, Warren Bennis (the guru of leadership studies and author of the afterword for this book), the process of becoming a leader is really the same as the process of becoming a full human being: each of us has to become the author of our own life, the maker of our own leadership.

Second, Betsy personifies the axiom that the best leaders are also the best listeners.

Some would-be leaders believe that if they just talk long enough, or even loudly enough, other people are bound to follow them. Not true: other people hit the mute button. The most accomplished leaders have found that if they listen closely to others—"deep listening," as Warren Bennis puts it—they can relate far more effectively to the dreams and fears of others. For some years, I watched as Bill Clinton would first enter an unfamiliar group. He would stop and talk intently to one individual after another, hearing their stories, learning about their families and friends, figuring out what made them tick. Only after he had immersed himself in the group would he step forward to speak or lead. He would capture the zeitgeist of the group and help give it voice. And, by the way, he had an astonishing memory. It is said that at the top of his game, Jack Nicklaus could remember almost every shot he had made in a championship golf tournament even many years earlier. Bill Clinton could remember every conversation—and every name.

Betsy is a leader very much in this tradition. As you read this book, you will find story upon story of conversations she has had with friends and acquaintances over the years—and in each case, she shows how intently she listened and learned from what she heard. Don't get me wrong: Betsy is a voluble person and spellbinding as a speaker. But her words come from a place of deep listening.

Third, Betsy practices the central message of this book: she leads through the power of feelings.

All leaders must have a well-developed capacity for critical thinking; good judgment and sound decision-making are crucial. But we know from an accumulating body of research, especially built around "emotional intelligence," that a leader's self-awareness and self-control, together with an acute awareness of others and accompanying social skills, matter much more than conventional wisdom has held. Daniel Goleman, whose work on EQ is widely read, has found that brains can often lift people into the C-Suite, but what then distinguishes them as good or bad executives depends heavily upon their ability to engage in relational leadership.

Betsy is a person of feelings—she has feelings for others and she can make others feel better about themselves. Years of experience in the arena have convinced her that this is the best path to leadership. Her website prominently displays one of her favorite quotes, drawn from Maya Angelou: "I've learned that people will forget what you said, people will forget what you did, but people will never forget how you made them feel."

I hope you enjoy and gain as much from these next pages as I have. I know that by the time you finish, you will learn what I have—that Betsy Myers is special.

TAKE THE LEAD

INTRODUCTION

A Road Map for Leadership

At a recent back-to-school night, I was chatting with one of my daughter's teachers. "Madison told me you are writing a book," she said. "What's it about?" I told her it was about leadership and how successful leaders bring out the most productive feelings in those around them. "Like what you do here with the kids in your class," I added.

"Oh," she mused, "I don't really see myself as a leader."

"Are you kidding?" I said. "You're teaching all these children how to read and write, how to share and other important life skills. They are growing and developing their sense of self-worth, and you are right in the middle of that process, teaching them how to learn and nurture their own abilities. You're leading them into their future!"

She looked surprised and thoughtful as she considered this idea. "I never thought of it like that," she said.

Most of us don't.

It's easy to view leadership as being something that relates only to the elite few. So often we see a "leader" as someone larger than life, as if leadership were something exclusive to powerful people in distant places: the CEO's suite or the general's tent, the pulpit or the podium. We tend to think of leadership in terms of grand

1

gestures and historic events: Washington crossing the Delaware, Lincoln issuing the Emancipation Proclamation, or Gandhi facing down the British Empire. But every CEO, general, or president starts as a child, with teachers and parents, coaches and friends who support and help shape them into the adult they will become.

LEADERSHIP IS EVERYWHERE

When my little sister JoJo was in first grade, her teacher was so mean to the kids that it often made her cry. This teacher ruled her classroom by fear and intimidation. She asked me once, "Why does your sister cry all the time?" I replied, "Because she's afraid of you!" No matter how I try, I cannot recall her name.

I have no trouble remembering my fifth-grade teacher's name. Hugh Beaton loved kids and loved teaching. Where JoJo's teacher would hover like a hawk, waiting to catch her pupils doing something wrong, Mr. Beaton always managed to catch us doing something right. He let us know he believed in us, and being in his presence brought out the best in us.

As the years passed and I encountered other teachers and mentors like Mr. Beaton, I have been fascinated by this mysterious quality these people seem to have in common.

What exactly *is* this thing we call leadership?

Why is it that some people challenge us and motivate us to rise to our best abilities, while others seem to drain our energy and spirit? What is that particular quality certain people have that causes those around them to engage fully and feel connected?

All my life I have been curious about this. What is leadership all about? How and when does it work? This curiosity has led me through careers in the worlds of business, academia, and political life.

Working in the Clinton White House, I would observe cabinet secretaries and senior staff with fascination. Why was it that Treasury Secretary Bob Rubin could walk down the halls of the White House and people would practically bow in respect, while another cabinet secretary would elicit nowhere near the same response? Why are some places such great places to work, while others feel grueling? Why does one department head or business executive inspire her people to greatness, while another evokes only apathy and disinterest from the ranks? Why is it that one teacher is beloved by students, while another is loathed and feared? What is that magical quality that brings out the best in people, and is it a secret known only by a precious few or something available to us all?

This book is my effort to address these questions. I don't claim to have discovered the exclusive "secret sauce" of leadership for the twenty-first century, because the answers to these questions have been here all along—but they are often missed or ignored. And I might well have missed them, too, but for the fact that I have been fortunate enough to have a front-row seat in some of our nation's most prestigious governmental, academic, and business institutions, offering me the chance to witness leadership success and failure in places large and small, public and private.

This is not a political book, although some of the stories and examples I'll share with you are drawn from my experiences in the Clinton White House and the 2008 Obama presidential campaign. It is not an academic book about leadership principles, although I'll also draw on experiences in the academic world, where I served as executive director of the Center for Public Leadership at Harvard's John F. Kennedy School of Government. Along with stories from these times, we'll also explore examples from friends and colleagues in the business world and insights gained through life with my family.

From what I've observed, genuine leadership is not something that magically happens because we've been handed a certain position or role to play. It is a quality we nurture in ourselves, regardless of our job or station in life. It is a function not of title, academic degrees, or access to power, but of how we treat and connect with the people around us.

I believe this magical quality *is* available to all of us, although it is often counterintuitive and quite different from what we may have been taught, or come to believe, true leadership looks like.

Many of us don't see ourselves as leaders, but the truth is that we are all confronted constantly with opportunities to *take the lead*. Whether we are managing a division of a company, interacting in our community, participating in a PTO or church organization, or raising our children, the way we feel about ourselves and treat others has an impact that adds or detracts, inspires or deflates. That takes the lead, or fails to do so.

From the Oval Office to the playground, whether in private life or public, in the home or workplace, in our communities and organizations, friendships and relationships, it's exactly the same principles at play. Leadership doesn't happen only on mountaintops and in summit meetings—leadership is *everywhere*.

A LEADERSHIP CRISIS

In the summer of 1999, I left the Clinton administration to pursue a master's in public administration at the John F. Kennedy School of Government at Harvard. Upon graduating in 2000 I joined the Kennedy School administration as director of Alumni and External Relations, and three years later I was recruited by David Gergen, director of the Center for Public Leadership at the Kennedy School, to take a position there as executive director.

There couldn't have been a more perfect job for me at the time. My position at the center offered an academic dimension to my years of experiential learning about leadership and allowed me to make this my full-time passion and occupation.

Harvard prides itself on being the premier institution in the world for the training of the world's leaders, whether in education, medicine, government, or business. The Center for Public Leadership was created in 2000, by a generous endowment from the businessman and philanthropist Les Wexner (owner of The Limited and Victoria's Secret) and his wife, Abigail, with a mandate to focus on research, curricula, and teaching, both inside and outside the classroom, on leadership thought and practice. The next few years at the center provided a rare opportunity to meet and work with some of our country's top leadership experts from business, academia, and government, as well as graduate students from all over the world, bringing a broader perspective and sharper focus to my fascination with leadership. I was especially interested in exploring a new kind of leadership—one that the new century required.

When I began working as the center's executive director in the fall of 2003, it was evident that trust in our leaders had been steadily declining in every sector nationwide, and it seemed that this prevailing sense of distrust had been deepening for well more than a decade.

Warren Bennis, the distinguished scholar and dean of American leadership who also served as our board chairman, suggested that we undertake an annual study to identify how ordinary Americans viewed the current state of leadership, both generally and across all the professions, and to track these trends over the next several years.

In the summer of 2004, at the Democratic Convention in Boston, David Gergen and I met with the publisher and the editor of the *U.S. News & World Report (USNWR)*: Bill Holiber and Brian Kelly. We pitched the idea of teaming up to conduct an annual survey of attitudes on leadership and creating a report to be published jointly, with a special issue of their magazine devoted to identifying the nation's best leaders. The following spring the project was launched, and that October we published the results of our first annual *National Leadership Index*, titled "A National Study of Confidence in Leadership." (The *Index* and special issue of *USNWR* have continued publication every year since.)

The numbers were alarming, though hardly surprising. We were able to verify that, yes, public confidence in leadership had seen a twenty-year decline, and that two-thirds (66 percent) of Americans felt we were mired in a leadership crisis. Nearly three-quarters (72 percent) of them believed that unless the country's leaders improved, the United States would decline as a nation. Americans across all categories of age, geography, gender, and political affiliation were not confident that their leaders would respond effectively in a crisis, such as a natural disaster or a terrorist attack.[1]

This deficiency was felt at the highest levels of government as well as in most other sectors of society, including education and business. The only places where our leaders garnered even a "moderate" level of confidence (and even here just barely) were

---

1. These numbers had declined further by the time of our 2006 report, and even further by the 2007 report.

in medicine and our military. The lowest-rated leadership of all
was in the media. Our data showed that we were in the throes of a
full-fledged leadership crisis. From our homes and families, to our
churches, mosques, and synagogues, to our workplaces and halls of
government, Americans were deeply disappointed in their leaders.

Since the publication of our first *Index*, the numbers have only
grown worse.

Not surprisingly, this crisis in leadership has brought with it a
parallel crisis in the workforce. Polls and studies indicate that as
many as 70 percent of American workers report feeling "not engaged" or "actively disengaged" at work. It seems that poor leadership makes for unhappy and disaffected people.

In addition to the enormous toll this takes on the human spirit
and such intangibles as family and personal happiness, there are
also mind-boggling economic costs involved. According to one
study, disengagement and low morale in the workplace create an
economic burden of some $350 billion annually in the US alone,
with similar impact occurring in other countries around the world.[2]

A NEW ERA OF LEADERSHIP

The leadership crisis documented in the *Index* was not simply about
the particular individuals who happened to be in positions of power
at the time. Something bigger and deeper was going on. We had
entered a new era, one that required a new leadership paradigm.

There was a time when the classic command-and-control style

---

2. Robin Athey, "It's 2008: Do You Know Where Your Talent Is?" Deloitte Development, 2004.

of leadership worked, but what worked then doesn't work now. The
world has changed in the past two decades, in profound and permanent
ways. Society has grown more diverse, with the younger generation,
women, and minorities playing a far more central role. According to
the US Department of Labor, by 2008 seven in every ten new entrants
into the workforce were women and people of color.[3]

One of the most intriguing results from our first annual *Index*
was that the majority of those surveyed felt the country would be
better off with more women in leadership positions.

Why?

One reason surely is the increasing presence of women in the
workforce: by 2010, the number of women in the US labor force
actually outnumbered men. Yet I believe there is another, more
central reason. Women tend to bring a very different dynamic to
leadership, one that is collaborative and team-centered, that thrives
on connection, relationship, openness, and cooperation with those
who have different viewpoints and beliefs. This is a kind of leadership that does not simply direct or manage people but *engages* them.

Since the experiences and views that inform these pages are
mine, *Take the Lead* naturally reflects a woman's reality and point
of view. Yet it is not my intention to write a book for women alone
but for everyone who shares my fascination with leadership, regardless of the individual leader's gender. These are the qualities of
leadership, I believe, that are central to what our new era demands
and that today's leaders, both men and women, need to embrace.

In the traditional corporate world, the focus was about going
up the ladder. People would enter the workforce and be with the
same company for forty years. Not anymore. The pace of change

---

3. Aon Hewitt, "Preparing for the Workforce of Tomorrow," February 2004.

has dramatically accelerated and society has become incredibly fluid and mobile. The Internet has transformed social and economic patterns as radically as electricity and the automobile did in the early twentieth century, giving people a voice in a way that was not possible only a generation ago. Today, people expect and even demand more out of their lives—and their workplaces. We want more participation in decisions. We want to have an impact, to live a more purposeful and values-centered life, and to be acknowledged for doing so. The emerging need is not simply for *better* leadership but for a new *kind* of leadership, one based on listening, transparency, and a fundamental honoring of relationships. As we are seeing in the Middle East and Africa in early 2011, people everywhere are demanding to have a voice.

In the spring of 2006, six months after the release of our first annual *National Index,* we convened a special conference at the center, titled "Growing Leaders in a Changing World," to explore these issues. The conference's theme was also chosen to honor the life and work of our board chairman, Warren Bennis, who had just turned eighty-one.

Warren is unique among leadership authorities in that his work has been influential in academic circles as well as in business and the popular literature. Among his dozens of works, Warren's classic 1989 book, *On Becoming a Leader,* has served (and continues to serve) as the bible of leadership to several generations of American leaders.

The conference brought together the top experts in leadership from three vastly different worlds: academia, business, and popular thought. On the program, for example, were such respected academics as Max Bazerman, Hannah Riley Bowles, Ron Heifetz, Rosabeth Moss Kanter, Barbara Kellerman, Rod Kramer, Joseph

Nye, Jeffrey Sonnenfeld, and Noel Tichy, sharing the dais with such popular bestselling authors as Ken Blanchard (*The One Minute Manager*), Stephen Covey (*The 7 Habits of Highly Effective People*), Tom Peters (*In Search of Excellence*), Harvey Mackay (*Swim with the Sharks Without Being Eaten Alive*), John Kotter (*Our Iceberg Is Melting*), and Spencer Johnson (*Who Moved My Cheese?*). Adding yet another dimension to the proceedings was a long list of extremely successful and influential business leaders, including Steve Belkin (Trans National Group Services), Bill George (Medtronic), Georgette Mosbacher (Borghese), Howard Schultz (Starbucks), Jack Welch (GE), and Les Wexner (Limited Brands). Rounding out the roster were such leadership authorities as Brian Duffy, editor of *U.S. News & World Report*, former governor Michael Dukakis, Eric Shinseki, former chief of staff of the US Army, and Admiral Thad Allen, commandant of the US Coast Guard.

It was a remarkably distinguished who's who of contemporary leadership, a rare combination of political and business experience with leading academic researchers and popular bestselling authors, known as *thought leaders*, all under the same roof. In essence, it was a collective state of the union address on leadership in America and what is needed for the new century.

What made the conference even more remarkable was that all these diverse authorities were describing essentially the same picture. There was a new kind of leadership afoot, said the conferees, a leadership of the mind *and* the heart. This new paradigm emphasized such traits as authenticity, collaboration, and caring.

"As leaders, we are all angels with only one wing," Warren said in his concluding remarks that evening. "We can fly—but only if we embrace each other."

The Harvard conference echoed the experiences and observations I'd had over the decades and further validated my own ideas about leadership, which boil down to these three fundamental beliefs:

- Leadership is a function first and foremost of self-knowledge and honest self-reflection.

- Secondly, leaders don't always have all the answers. In fact, the strength of their leadership comes from their willingness to ask the questions.

- Finally, and most importantly, leaders draw their effectiveness less from what they know or what power they wield, and more from how they make the people around them feel.

LEADERSHIP STARTS WITH OURSELVES

Warren Bennis laid the groundwork for this view of leadership twenty years ago. He was the first to clearly articulate the understanding that leadership *is* self-knowledge.

At the time, most academics and researchers were still looking for that elusive magic formula, as if to say, "If leaders will just follow these five steps or imitate the actions of that particular Fortune 50 CEO, they will surely find success." But it doesn't work that way. Leadership isn't something you can put on like a suit of clothes or generate by copying someone else. Leadership is about who you genuinely *are*.

Successful leaders are those who are conscious about their behavior and the impact it has on the people around them. These leaders are willing to step back from the fray and get an accurate picture of what is working in their organizations—and in their lives—and what is not. Moreover, they want to know the *why*. They are willing to examine what behaviors of their own may be getting in the way. Successful leaders understand that if we don't lead consciously, it's easy to repeat patterns that could be keeping us from achieving the results we are hoping for.

The toughest person you will ever lead is yourself. We can't effectively lead others unless we can lead ourselves, which starts with knowing who we are.

LEADERS DON'T ALWAYS HAVE THE ANSWERS— BUT THEY ALWAYS HAVE THE QUESTIONS

Many of us grew up thinking that leaders and other authority figures had all the answers. But nobody can possibly know everything about every issue in the organization, business, school, or family they lead.

I have seen people shy away from leadership because they thought that to be the leader, they needed to have it all figured out from the start. In reality, it is very much the opposite. Effective leaders often don't have all the answers, and don't pretend to. What makes them leaders is that they are willing to ask the questions. They are *curious* about other perspectives, of both the experts and the people in the trenches, knowing that the answers are often right in our midst. And they are *generous* with what they learn and share it with others, devoting their own energies to helping others achieve success.

The old-fashioned command-and-control leadership style sees this sort of thinking as a weakness, but the new kind of leader knows that being open and asking questions is a strength that includes and motivates others. Effective leaders make it a priority in their schedules to get to know their community, seeking out the knowledge and experiences of their team members, constituents, colleagues, and family members, and giving credit where it is due.

LEADERSHIP IS ABOUT FEELINGS

Advanced degrees, years of experience, an important title, or access to power do not guarantee that you will be a successful leader. Leadership is about how you make people *feel*—about you, about the project or work you're doing together, and especially about *themselves*.

Why? Because people do their best work when they feel good about themselves and what they're doing. When people feel valued, appreciated, heard, supported, acknowledged, and included, they are motivated to bring their best selves forward. This is how initiatives get launched, profits are made, and the work gets done. It's not just about being nice, it is about being effective.

Most of us don't think of feelings as being the key to leadership success. It seems almost counterintuitive. But think for a moment about the times in your life when you have been most productive: were those also the times when you felt the most valued, supported, and appreciated?

LEADERSHIP IN THE TRENCHES

In January 2007, I left the center to take a position as chief operations officer for Barack Obama's presidential campaign, which was just getting under way. For the rest of that year I worked at the Chicago headquarters, building and managing the campaign's national operational infrastructure, which gave me a big-view, top-down frame of reference for the campaign's operation. However, the following year gave me the opportunity to gain a very different perspective. After transitioning in late 2007 from COO to become the chair of Women for Obama (WFO), I spent the next year gaining a very grassroots, in-the-trenches view of the campaign effort.

Sleeping in motels and driving rental cars, I crisscrossed many of the campaign battleground states during much of 2008, working side by side with staff and volunteers of all ages and from all backgrounds, witnessing firsthand the participation and dedication of these field organizers and staffers, donors, volunteers, and voters. It was this second, more ground-level perspective that showed me the true heart of this campaign.

Everywhere I traveled, the scene was the same: hundreds of people fully engaged and tirelessly devoted to their shared goal. These people had not been enticed with big expense accounts, cushy salaries, or public recognition. It was quite the opposite. Most of them had taken precious time away from their jobs, their families, and their careers, working for little or no pay, to knock on doors, stuff envelopes, and commit their time to mobilizing perfect strangers, often in towns and states they had never visited before.

It was in these hundreds and thousands of people on the ground that I saw some of the most powerful examples of what it looks like when people feel connected and passionate about what they are doing—and the results those feelings can bring about.

Regardless of your own political views, it is hard not to appreciate what this candidate and campaign accomplished in two short years. At the beginning of 2007, Senator Obama had less than 20 percent national name recognition and no endorsements to speak of—and twenty-two months later he was elected to become the nation's first African-American president. And this historic accomplishment was due largely to the enthusiastic staff and volunteers across the country, many of whom had never been involved in a political campaign before.

Most businesses and organizations dream about this kind of engagement, and would give anything (and *pay* anything) to generate that kind of participation and commitment from their people. How do you create that kind of experience? What causes people to bring that kind of energy and dedication to an organization or project? Was the Obama campaign an anomaly, or can that same level of passionate engagement be created in other organizations and companies?

During that year in the campaign I reflected on these questions every day, and whether I was in Montana or Rhode Island, the answers were amazingly similar. People got involved and stayed involved because they felt included and empowered to have a voice. They felt their contributions were valued and appreciated. They felt they were a connected part of something bigger than themselves.

Can that kind of powerful, committed engagement be replicated in other organizations? From what I've seen, it absolutely can.

This book is organized around seven core ideas:

    authenticity
    connection
    respect
    clarity
    collaboration
    learning
    courage

These seven qualities are not a magic formula or paint-by-numbers recipe, but they do provide a road map to effective leadership. Whether you are leading a class of kindergarteners, a team of employees, or a committee in Congress, these seven principles will help you bring out productive feelings in yourself and in those around you, while addressing and dealing with conflict in the healthiest and most constructive way.

The pages that follow trace these seven qualities through my encounters with everyday people, in places big and small, who have touched my heart with their leadership example.

It seems to me that our core desire to feel valued in our companies and organizations is not so different from the way we all want to feel valued in our families and relationships. In fact, it's not different at all. Whether you are sitting with your child in the playground or championing a new policy initiative in the White House, it's the same. We are all human. And perhaps deeper than any other human need is our desire to feel that we *matter*. It is in those moments of connection that people become inspired and motivated to take the lead and collaborate with you rather than remain passive observers or even struggle against you. It is in those moments of passionate engagement that we rise to our greatest abilities and proudest accomplishments, bringing out the best in ourselves and everyone around us.

1. AUTHENTICITY

Freaking Out with Joy

When she was four years old, my daughter, Madison, often saw her friends leaving their after-school program to go to soccer, ballet, piano, and other activities. One day, when I picked her up from preschool, she said, "Mommy, please don't overschedule me. I just want to play after school and relax on weekends!"

I said, "Okay, tell you what: I'll suggest some activities now and then, and when you're ready to do something outside of school, you can choose."

A few years later, when she was six, we went together to her best friend Rachael's dance recital. The program featured ballet, tap, jazz, and hip-hop for girls from three to twenty years old. It was a three-hour production—and Madison sat on the edge of her seat the whole time, completely enthralled in every minute of it.

"Mommy," she said after the recital was over, "*this* is what I want to do! Can we sign up right now?" So we did—she signed up for a class that combined ballet, tap, and jazz for her age group.

Sometime later, we went shopping for a leotard and shoes in preparation for her dance class. After Madison picked out a few different styles, we made our way to the fitting room, where she tried on each one to see which felt most comfortable. Finally, she made her choice: sleeveless and black with a matching skirt.

As she stood in front of the mirror, assessing her new outfit, her face lit up. "Mommy," she exclaimed, "I am freaking out with joy! I was *born* to dance!"

That was three years ago. Madison has since danced in several recitals herself, and she is totally engaged in her dance class. In fact, it has become her favorite part of the week. She prepares her dance bag the night before each class session to make sure she doesn't forget anything the next morning. After her first spring recital, when the dance studio shut down for summer recess, Madison said, "How am I going to live this summer without dance class? Dance is my life!" Ask her what she wants to be when she grows up and she replies without hesitation, "A dancer!" If you're looking for Madison, chances are good you'll find her in some part of the house practicing her dancing.

Madison's love of dancing reminds me that it is those times in our lives when we are *freaking out with joy* that give us the greatest clues about who we are and where we genuinely belong.

There is a unique, almost magnetic quality I've often noticed in people who wholeheartedly love what they do, and over the years I've come to recognize that quality as *authenticity*. When Madison is dancing, she is not only genuinely happy, she is also being fully *Madison*.

THERE ARE NO *IDEAL* LEADERS, ONLY *REAL* LEADERS

My neighbor Brian is a Latin teacher and track coach at a nearby high school; his wife, Mary, teaches middle school. Brian and I were talking one day about what it means to live authentically.

"You know," he said, "I really have no ambitions to do anything more than what I do right now. I enjoy teaching, and it gives me a lifestyle that allows me to work in the garden with Mary on weekends and do projects on the house in the summer."

Brian is clear about who he is and what makes him happy. In a word, he is *authentic*. Not surprisingly, his students love him and many stay in touch with him long after they've graduated.

Like Brian's students, we are naturally drawn to people who have an honest sense of themselves and are comfortable in their own skins. People who are authentic don't feel the need to exaggerate their story to make themselves look better, or to treat others poorly so they come out on top. They don't put energy into trying to imitate others or pretend to be anything other than who they are.

In Warren Bennis's book *On Becoming a Leader*, he says, "People begin to be leaders at that moment when they decide for themselves how to be."

"During the past 50 years," say Bill George and Peter Sims in *True North: Discover Your Authentic Leadership*, "leadership scholars have conducted more than 1,000 studies in the attempt to determine the definitive styles, characteristics, or personality traits of great leaders. None of these studies has produced a clear profile of the ideal leader."

This is not a failure of scholarship. In fact, it is an example of excellent scholarship, and what it demonstrates with such scientific thoroughness is that there *is* no clear profile of "the ideal leader." Genuine leadership is not about trying to imitate another leader or striving to fit into a certain box or definition. Genuine leadership is what emerges when we are fully and freely ourselves.

"I have often thought," wrote the philosopher William James, "that the best way to define a man's character would be to seek out the particular mental or moral attitude in which, when it came upon him, he felt himself most deeply and intensively active and alive. At such moments, there is a voice inside which speaks and says, 'This is the real me!'" [1]

Do you feel passionate about your work? Do you regularly find yourself freaking out with joy? Life is short. We should spend it doing something we love—something that fully and truly expresses who we are.

This is not to say that the activity, situation, or career that fits is necessarily easy or trouble free. Doing what we love can be challenging. In fact, it often is. But when it's right, even if it may be difficult, it's *right*—and we know it. In those moments when things feel *right*, when I am *freaking out with joy* at what I'm doing, I feel both excited and peaceful. It feels like I'm being true to myself. This quote (from an anonymous author) on the nature of being at peace perfectly captures this feeling of authenticity:

"It does not mean to be in a place where there is no noise, trouble, or hard work. It means to be in the midst of those things and still be calm in your heart."

President Clinton said much the same thing one day, albeit in different words. I had asked him how he was able to deal with negative press when it came his way.

"Betsy," he said, "I love my job on the worst of days." He truly did, and his joy was infectious, just as Brian's sense of contentment and Madison's love of dancing are infectious.

Authenticity boils down to finding "the real me" in each of us. When we know who we are, others can sense that about us, and are far more likely to trust our leadership.

---

1. William James to his wife, Alice Gibbens James, in 1878, in *The Letters of William James* (Atlantic Monthly Press, Boston, 1920), 199.

MEETING BARACK OBAMA

I met Barack Obama for the first time in 2005, when David Gergen and I took a group of about two dozen Harvard students to Washington for our annual Zuckerman Fellowship trip. Funded by Mort Zuckerman, the owner of *U.S. News & World Report,* this program is for students who are pursuing joint degrees in public policy along with business, law, or medicine, and are keenly interested in learning what goes on in Washington. Over a period of three days, the students have the opportunity to meet Hill staff, people from think tanks and government posts, press, and members of Congress.

For this year's trip, a fifteen-minute visit with Senator Obama was on our agenda, and I was curious about what words of wisdom he would share in his brief moments with the students. I remember thinking it hadn't been that long ago that he had been here himself, as a Harvard Law student.

The group sat down in the senator's office, and a few minutes later he walked in with a big smile and welcomed the students enthusiastically. He launched into a story about his 2000 congressional campaign, sharing with them what it had felt like to lose that race to incumbent Bobby Rush, about the mistakes he had made and how much the experience had humbled him.

"And it got worse," he admitted. "When I tried to get to Los Angeles to attend the Democratic Convention, I got only as far as the Chicago airport—and my credit card was declined." The senator looked around at the two dozen faces. "Not only was I broke, but my wife was really mad at me."

The students laughed, and he laughed too.

"It was a low point in my life. But here I am, five years later, a US senator."

His message was clear: we all skin our knees; what counts is how we pick ourselves up, learn from our mistakes, and move forward.

It struck me that he could have spent those minutes talking about his life as a senator or discussing policy or legislative matters. He could have wowed these students with stories of his successes at the *Harvard Law Review,* in the Illinois legislature, or on the Chicago streets as a community organizer. Instead, he shared with them about a time in his life when he had failed.

It struck me how comfortable he was in his own skin. He knew who he was, and he was not trying to be anyone else.

THE TRAIT THAT MATTERED MOST

A year and a half later, I found myself going to work for Senator Obama's presidential campaign as chief operations officer. There was something about his leadership style that intrigued me. It was less about whether he would win or lose the race and more about the possibility of offering the world a different picture of how a leader behaves, with his message about civility, collaboration, compromise, and embracing our commonality. This was the message of his speech at the Democratic Convention in 2004. Was this who he really was, I wondered, and if so, what would that look like on the national political stage?

It was an intriguing opportunity—and I also knew it was a job that would turn my life upside down. It would mean leaving my position at the Kennedy School, a job I loved and that still offered much growth, as well as leaving my husband, Rob, and our 4½-year-old daughter for long stretches of time.

There's a reason most campaign staffers are in their twenties.

Political campaigns are a demanding business, an exhausting, all-out marathon. Young people can handle those twenty-hour days for months on end, living on nothing but coffee, junk food, and the adrenaline provided by news (whether good or bad) from the latest poll results. It's all part of the excitement. I'd been there: I'd worked on campaign staffs in my twenties, and had been at the White House during President Clinton's 1996 reelection campaign. But my life was different now, and there was no denying how difficult this could be on my family—how could I say yes? But I believed it could be an extraordinary moment for our country—how could I say no?

What tipped the scales and made my decision clear was the fact that Senator Obama seemed to embody a number of key leadership traits that I felt the world needed, and especially this: *he was authentic.*

At a senior staff planning meeting in Washington a few weeks later, Obama made a statement that crystallized for me that this had been the right decision.

"I know this will be a long road," said the senator, now candidate, to the twenty of us seated around the table. "If I am who I am and we win, great. And if I am who I am and we lose, then so be it. But don't ask me to change who I am to win this thing."

Barack Obama was who he said he was, and that *mattered.*

KNOWING YOUR OWN STORY

One person who played a pivotal (although largely anonymous) role in the Obama campaign is Marshall Ganz, a rumpled, teddy-bearish Harvard professor with an amazing gift for communicating and facilitating. Marshall and I had crossed paths at the Kennedy

School, where he was both respected and beloved for his experience and his teaching about political and community organizing.
As with his students, he quickly developed a similar reputation
among our young field organizers.

Marshall first learned about community organizing in the early
1960s while working with the civil rights movement in Mississippi.
In his first political campaign he led a group of migrant farmwork-
ers in 1968 in an effort to get out the vote for Bobby Kennedy.
Most of the people he worked with were not citizens and could not
vote themselves—but they could work to get others out to vote.
And under Marshall's tutelage and inspiration, they did just that:
the East LA region where he worked had a primary turnout that
topped an amazing 80 percent.

According to Marshall, creating an effective movement starts
with and hinges on telling your own story—and that depends on
knowing your own story. Says Marshall:

"There has to be a *me* before there can be a *me and you*.
Relationships are not about losing yourself; they are about *claiming*
yourself in such a way that you can enter into a relationship with
someone else.

"By learning to tell your own story—who you are and what
drew you here—you will be able to hear the stories of others in
such a way that you can make an *us* out of a *me*. And then you've
got the power to act, which is where it needs to go. The real core of
what these stories teach goes to the heart, not to the head."

Working with our state organizers, Marshall developed a storytelling format for training volunteers and campaign workers. Each
gathering would begin by having everyone in the group share a bit
about their own life story. He conducted dozens of these sessions
around the country.

This is quite different from the conventional campaign training format. Rather than talking *at* the assembled group and telling
them about the issues that mattered to the candidate and the campaign, Marshall went about it from the other direction. He started
out by asking people to tell us about what mattered to *them* and
why they had taken the time to come to the meeting. By sharing
their stories with each other from the very beginning, the people
who attended these sessions felt more connected to the campaign
and to each other in a genuine, personal way. As Marshall put it,
these gatherings became an opportunity to "go from me to us," and
from there to "what we can do together."

WILL THE REAL CANDIDATE PLEASE STAND UP?

The importance of "knowing your own story" turned out to be
even more important to our campaign than most of us could have
predicted, because in a way, the 2008 presidential contest became a
referendum on authenticity.

In the 1930s, FDR pioneered the use of radio as a communication tool with his famous "fireside chats," and it was through
his voice on broadcast that he maintained his connection with the
American people through the difficult years of economic hardship
and the run-up to World War II. JFK was the first television president. But both radio and television are selective media, that is, you
can choose when to show up and strategize carefully how to put
your best foot forward.

Not so with the Internet. In the age of bloggers and inexpen-
sive handheld digital video cameras, you are always *on*, whether or
not you are aware of it or prepared for it—as Virginia senator and

presidential hopeful George Allen's supporters discovered to their dismay, when Allen's promising presidential campaign fizzled in the summer of 2006. A camcorder caught him ridiculing an Indian-American volunteer worker for one of his opponents as "this fellow here with the yellow shirt, macaca, or whatever his name is." Within minutes the footage was on the web, and Allen's prospects for a presidential bid were over.

Obama campaigned in an era when the Internet brought a new level of total exposure to the world, an Age of Authenticity in which, courtesy of blogs, podcasts, online streaming video, and other social media, the distinction between public persona and private person is all but gone. Those of us who spoke on the campaign trail on behalf of our candidate soon grew accustomed to having our speeches show up within hours on YouTube.

The 2008 general election presented the nation with two candidates who had already told their own stories authentically: Barack Obama and John McCain.

John McCain's story is certainly as compelling as Barack Obama's: the wounded prisoner of war who refused repatriation ahead of his fellow prisoners; the maverick politician willing to buck the trends and disagree with his Republican colleagues; the political reformer who challenged business as usual and called to task his fellow senators on both sides of the aisle. In fact, one of the things that most endeared people to McCain was his realness. With his plainspoken, what-you-see-is-what-you-get quality, he garnered fans from both political parties. In his 2000 presidential primary campaign, McCain invited the press to sit with him on his bus, the Straight Talk Express, and they loved it. This unprecedented access allowed them to build a rapport with the senator and their coverage reflected it.

Then, in 2008, as we began heading into the general election, something happened: it seemed as if McCain had lost track of his authentic self. McCain the man and McCain the presidential candidate started becoming two separate things. He became more stiff and scripted, playing the part of the party candidate rather than the genuine maverick reformer that had endeared him to so many. People began wondering what was real and what was a gimmick. It was as if the McCain candidacy was present and accounted for, but McCain the person had disappeared from view.

Obama stayed Obama, but McCain stopped being McCain— and I believe that became one of the most compelling factors in the election's outcome. On the evening of Election Day, many people had the same reaction to Senator McCain's concession speech as I did: "Oh, *there* he is!" It was his most authentic speech of the campaign, simply speaking from his heart. Unfortunately for him, it came several months too late.

In both the 2000 and 2004 elections, on the other hand, George W. Bush was clear about who he was and what he stood for. I believe that he won a second term because, like him or not, agree with him or not, the American people felt they knew who he was. What struck me as even more fascinating about the 2000 election, though, was what happened to Bush's opponent, Al Gore—*after* the election was over.

With the campaign behind him, former vice president Gore stepped squarely into his role as leading authority on the environment, which was where his heart and passion were. The respect he garnered throughout the world in the following years was remarkable, and it spoke to who he was. I have no doubt that he would have been a successful president, but his contributions to the environment, along with his place on the world stage, have had significant impact that may long outlast the four or eight years he would have had in the Oval Office. Within the few short years following his bid for the presidency, he had won an Emmy, an Academy Award, a Grammy, and a Nobel Peace Prize for his book and documentary film *An Inconvenient Truth*. Al Gore was living his authentic life, and the world opened its arms in support.

When you step into who you truly are, you access a source of inexhaustible power. People see you as *real*, and that causes them to feel a level of trust and confidence that no amount of spin or PR can possibly manufacture.

My friend Annie McLane Kuster is a perfect example of someone who has embraced her authentic self in a public position. Annie was one of the Obama campaign's earliest volunteers in New Hampshire and chair of the Women for Obama efforts there. After the 2008 election, Annie's deep involvement with the campaign and her personal commitment to public service inspired her to run for Congress.

Annie was in Boston in the summer of 2009 to meet with supporters and we met for lunch. As she shared her campaign plans, our conversation turned to the topic of authentic leadership.

"Women generally have some insecurity, whether it's hidden or they wear it on their sleeves," Annie commented. "*I wish I was taller, I wish I was thinner, I wish I was smarter,* whatever it might be. We go through our lives like that, and it probably happens for men, too.

"But rather than focusing on what I'm not, I've learned that the more authentic I am, the better response I have from people. It's such a simple thing. If I am just myself—completely, authentically, one hundred percent myself—*that's* what people respond to."

She related a conversation she'd had that morning with a lawyer friend.

"I told him I was thinking about growing out my hair and getting rid of my glasses. He gave me a huge hug and said, 'Annie, do *not* let them change anything about you. Just be yourself! That's who needs to go to Congress—you!'"

Annie talked about how easy it is to get lost in trying to please others or live up to their expectations. But as she pointed out, people trust us when we are genuine—when we show up, not as who we think we should be, not who our parents and teachers, colleagues and bosses say we should be, but as who we really *are*.

In the 2010 election, when the entire state swung strongly to the Republican side, Annie lost to Republican Charles Bass by a margin of one point. I have no doubt she will one day be a member of Congress.

TAKING THE TIME TO LISTEN TO OURSELVES

The challenge of authenticity is that it is not a switch you can simply turn on at will. Just as any meaningful relationship with another person needs time to invest and nurture, our relationship with *ourselves* also takes time to develop.

We all grow up in a context where we are pushed and pulled by a whole host of social influences—parents, teachers, and other figures of authority who encourage us to be one way, friends who urge us to be another way, millions of mixed messages from the media telling us to be all sorts of ways. "Where do I belong? What is the pearl I am adding to the world? Who am I, *really*?" These are questions that rarely come with easy answers.

From what I've seen, our level of self-awareness does not necessarily correlate with intelligence, education, or position. There are plenty of brilliant, well-educated, and highly placed people in the world who lack self-awareness.

How do we get that clarity on who we really are? It can feel hard to figure out and sometimes even harder to face, but I believe we *know* it instinctively. We know what it feels like when we're wearing a sweater that doesn't fit or doesn't match our personal style. Sometimes we decide to wear it anyway, but we know it's making us uncomfortable. If it feels like you're wearing the wrong sweater, you probably are.

We are each born with our own internal compass, an innate sense that tells us if the direction we're heading in feels right or doesn't feel right. Sometimes we ignore that gut feeling, or talk ourselves into believing it is steering us wrong. Most of us can remember times when we made poor choices because we didn't listen to our instincts.

Feedback from others can be valuable, even crucial, and it's important to have people in your life who know you and can give you that honest feedback. But the most important feedback is that which comes from ourselves. Part of living an authentic life is learning to trust that internal compass.

How do we learn to trust ourselves? It may take making the effort to create the space in our lives to step back and hear what our instincts are telling us. Today's world allows little time for quiet reflection. We easily find ourselves overscheduled, constantly multitasking, with information coming at us from a dozen different directions at once, all clamoring for our attention. When do we make the time to unplug and just be with ourselves for a while?

One reason I decided to enroll in a one-year master's program at the Kennedy School was to give myself time to reflect on all the experience I'd had during my time in the Clinton administration.

I wanted time to assess the lessons learned from those years in the fast-paced world of Washington, to explore what skills or other areas of my life I wanted to work on, and to decide how best to spend the next decade.

During that quiet year of classes, seminars, conversations, and alone time, I arrived at a few realizations. For one thing, it became clear that although politics and government appealed to me, it was really the leadership angle that bore the most interest for me. Without having taken that time to reflect and get in touch with my authentic passion for leadership, my career may never have taken the turn it has.

During that time I also realized that, while my career was important to me, so was having a family. I wanted to be a mother, and as I was nearing the end of my thirties, having a child had become a priority. I graduated at the end of that yearlong program on June 8—and on June 9, married my husband, Rob. Madison came along two years later.

Since that time I've learned that it doesn't have to take a full year to gain perspective. My friend Maggie Williams once told me she reserves Fridays for "thinking time." Today my unplugging consists of ninety minutes of yoga, which I try to do a few times a week. During those times, I put away my cell phone and put my brain on autopilot. It not only helps my health, it also helps my sanity—and it helps me stay in touch with my inner compass.

HELPING OTHERS STEP INTO WHO THEY ARE

Another influential thought leader I had the opportunity to meet at the Kennedy School was Jim Collins. In his book *Good to Great*,

Collins writes about the key traits of great companies and organizations. His research shows that such organizations are dedicated to making sure they have "the right people on the bus," as he puts it, as well as the wrong people *off* the bus. They also strive to make sure they have the right people in each seat, exercising their authentic talents and abilities. This is when organizations are at their best.

This idea has always resonated with me, and I've tried to follow this approach in every organization I have led. It is the leader's job to ensure that people are in the right seats—and on the right bus.

After joining David Gergen at the Center for Public Leadership, I spent my first few months there engaging the team in conversation—staff, students, faculty, everyone—to learn as much as possible about the center, its purpose and history. One staff person, whom I will call Susan, had been with the center since it first opened its doors in 2000.

An engaging, affable woman, Susan could often be found at the front desk, answering the phone or receiving guests. At first I assumed she was the receptionist, but I soon learned that her title was actually director of special projects.

As executive director, it was my responsibility to ensure that each staff member was in the right seat and that their position was right for their skills and abilities. As I discovered more about Susan's background, I was surprised to learn that she was a highly accomplished musician with five degrees in music, including two in piano performance and three in music theory and analysis. Her PhD from Goldsmiths College, the University of London, had been awarded magna cum laude in acknowledgment of her original research. She had authored two books on music theory. For twelve years she had been chair of music history at the Longy

School of Music in Cambridge. She had been giving preconcert talks to Boston Symphony Orchestra audiences at Symphony Hall since 2000. And here she was, fetching coffee for guests at our center's meetings!

It was no secret that Susan was in the wrong seat. It was also becoming clear that she was probably on the wrong bus.

There was an assumption among the staff that having a conversation regarding Susan's future would be unproductive, possibly leading to lawsuits or other unpleasant outcomes. But, as is so often the case in situations like this, no one had ever really examined this assumption or taken the time to discuss her future with her.

I had a conversation with Susan, asking her questions about her life in a way that made it clear that her job was not in jeopardy. Was she happy and fulfilled at the center? Given her impressive pedigree in music, I was genuinely curious about her hopes for her future. "What would your dream job be?" I asked her.

"Oh," she said, "I'd love to go back to teaching music at a university. But I don't know if that's a realistic goal. . . ."

She shared with me how the death of her husband had left her a single parent raising two teenage children. She needed to hold down a secure job with benefits.

The two of us continued to talk, and over the next few months we developed a plan that would allow her to look into possible jobs in the music field while staying fully employed at the center. Several months later, Susan was hired as associate professor of musicology and head of the music history department at a university in Florida, where she has been teaching ever since.

In her second year there, Susan was promoted; soon after that she was awarded an endowed faculty fellowship to teach abroad. Since being at her new post, she has flourished.

What happened to Susan is simple: she stepped into her authentic self. I talked with her not long ago by phone, and she said, "Betsy, you changed my life." But the truth is, I didn't. She just returned to her life's passion and to being who she really is.

GIVING YOURSELF PERMISSION TO CHANGE DIRECTION

Finding your place in the world isn't necessarily something you figure out one time and then have all worked out for the rest of your life. We continue discovering new things about ourselves throughout our lives and careers, and sometimes a situation that felt right for us at one point starts feeling like it's no longer a fit. Sometimes we need to be open to a change in plans and give ourselves permission to change direction.

This happened to me during the Obama campaign. In the fall of 2007, almost a year into my experience with the campaign, I found myself thinking about making a change. Working with organizations in the start-up or growth phase is a challenge I enjoy and has become an area of expertise for me. In the campaign's first days, we had started out without bank account, desks, or phones, with no central office and hardly any staff. Over the months that followed, we hired several hundred people and opened seventy offices throughout the early states (Iowa, New Hampshire, South Carolina, and Nevada). It was challenging, and it was fascinating.

But by that fall we had moved past the start-up phase and on to the day-to-day running of the campaign. The operations team was humming, and my days were now filled with budget meetings and logistics, contracts and data issues, personnel matters and vendor decisions. As a natural extrovert who loves interacting with people more than spreadsheets and contracts, I began to feel out of place. I was certainly not *freaking out with joy.*

It was just at this time that a new opportunity presented itself. We had started organizing our outreach to women voters under an umbrella we called Women for Obama, and given my past White House role as director of the Office for Women, this was a natural fit. Becoming chair of this organization offered a role that I sensed would energize me.

In late 2007, as the national chair of Women for Obama, I began traveling to the early states to work with our state staff in the trenches, speak at house parties and town halls, and participate in the effort to reach out to undecided voters, and especially women. I loved being out in the country with our young staff and meeting constituents. It was a role that was helpful to the state teams, and one where I felt more *me.* For much of 2008, it would become my full-time effort.

Sometimes you need to give yourself permission to change direction. This was a powerful lesson I learned as a teenager from my mom.

As a youth, my mother, Judy Burleigh, was an accomplished student. Earning the title of top Latin scholar in the Illinois high school system one year, she skipped a grade, graduated a year early, and enrolled in the University of Wisconsin. That year, as a seventeen-year-old freshman with a history of straight As, she met and fell in love with my father, a handsome fifth-year senior named Steve Myers.

Following his passion for aviation, my dad enrolled in navy flight school after graduation, which took him to Newport, Rhode Island. Like so many other women of her generation, at the age of nineteen my mother put her future on hold. Dropping out of college, she married my father and moved east with him.

Four short years later, now barely twenty-three, my mother found herself managing a household including her husband and three little girls. I had come along first, followed a year later by my sister Dee Dee and our sister Mary Jo (JoJo) the year after that. For the next decade plus, my mom raised us and supported my father's career, doing what women did in those times: burying her dreams in favor of her husband's.

From the moment she left the University of Wisconsin–Madison, my mother had always planned to finish her degree, but with the constant moves involved in my father's navy career, she had only managed to take a few classes here and there. By her early thirties, things had begun to settle down a bit. My father had left the navy and now worked for Lockheed Aircraft Corporation in Burbank, California. Not only was there more stability in her life but the three of us girls were now tweens with busy lives of our own—and so my mother decided it was time to return to school.

She enrolled at California State University at Northridge, and for the next two years attended school full time, majoring in psychology. After finishing her undergraduate degree, she went on to get a master's in psychology. At the same time, she began working part time at Oxnard Community College, where she ran a program for women looking to reenter the workforce. Many of these women were single mothers with few resources or little job experience. She also recruited women to return to school, helping them see how their life experiences could become the basis for job skills. My mother was the perfect person for this job, because she had just done the same thing they were doing.

My mother's decision to reach for her authentic self had a profound impact on me. She shifted the dynamics in our family, and we all stepped up, including my father, to support her. By her actions, she taught me that we each have the power to determine or change our roles in both our personal and professional lives. She shifted my view of what was possible. By standing up for herself, she stood up for my sisters and me. By gaining her own voice, she gave *us* voice.

Most of all, she showed me how important it is to create your authentic life, even if it upsets the status quo and is challenging to pursue.

"I loved that time in my life," she told me recently as we reminisced about those early years. "I was so happy." Like Susan, she had stepped into who she truly was—and she was freaking out with joy.

How to Take the Lead

Authenticity simply means finding "the real me" within ourselves and being comfortable in our own skin. When you step into who you truly are, you access a source of inexhaustible power. People see you as *real*, and that causes them to feel a level of trust and confidence that no amount of spin or PR can possibly manufacture.

- Do you feel passionate about your work? Do you regularly find yourself *freaking out with joy*? These are often the times that give you the greatest clues about who you are and where you genuinely belong. Life is short. We should spend it doing something we love.

- Do you put energy into trying to live up to others' expectations? Do you feel yourself sometimes trying to be the person your parents, teachers, colleagues, bosses, employees, or others think you should be? Remember that people trust you most when you are genuine—when you show up as who you truly *are*.

- Do you regularly give yourself the time and space to listen to your own instinctive sense? Part of learning to trust your internal compass is allowing yourself the room to step back and hear what your instincts are telling you—to just *be* with yourself for a while.

- Do you feel you bring your authentic self to your relationship? The strongest relationships are not about losing yourself; they are about *claiming* yourself—which then makes it possible to enter into genuine relationships with others. As Marshall Ganz puts it, "There has to be a *me* before there can be a *me and you*."

- We continue discovering new things about ourselves throughout our lives and careers. Sometimes a situation that felt right at one point starts feeling like it's no longer a fit—and we need to *give ourselves permission to change direction.*

2. CONNECTION

The Story of Us

One morning a few years ago, as I was leaving for work, a green Buick pulled up in front of our house in the Boston suburb where we live. A tall, handsome gentleman in his early eighties got out of his car and asked if I lived here. Yes, I replied. He introduced himself. His name was Dick Husselbee, and he had lived in this house as a child with his mother, his aunt, and two cousins.

We chatted for a few minutes, and then I offered to show Mr. Husselbee the inside of the house. As we walked through each room, he regaled me with stories of the people who had lived there and what had changed since he was last there, which had been some sixty years earlier.

We went out back and he marveled at the large, beautiful oak tree in our backyard.

"This tree is one of our favorite things about the house," I told him.

He nodded. "It was just a stick then," he said with a smile.

He told me about a small trapdoor he and one of his cousins had made in a baseboard behind the door in one of the bedrooms to hide their jacks and other treasures. We went to that room and found, to his delight, that the tiny door was still there. I still smile every time I come across it. In honor of its history, we are leaving it intact.

As he was leaving, I invited him to come back sometime with the other members of his family who had lived in the house.

"Oh, Betsy," he said, "they are all gone." He paused in thought and remembrance, and then said, "This house was a place of love." I saw the tears in his eyes and realized that mine were tearing up, too. Incredibly, the family we bought this house from just four years earlier had said the exact same thing: *This house was a place of love.*

Dick Husselbee and I shared a connection to a house ("the 120," as he called it, referring to its street address), but the real connection was to what the house represented. There is a comfort in the sight, smells, and sounds that bring back cherished memories of a shared history. It is our sense of belonging, a link to who we are and to the people we love and who love us. Dick Husselbee was so strongly connected to those experiences that the echoes of times past were still vivid to him more than sixty years later.

These powerful bonds are the foundation of our humanity. It is no wonder that such moments linger for decades and still warm our hearts, even after all the years gone by.

THE POWER OF FEELING CONNECTED

Feeling connected to others is what gives our lives meaning and fuels our sense of belonging. A sense of connection can come from a shared passion, a shared experience or history, a shared goal or mission. It speaks to our desire to identify with and feel part of something bigger than ourselves. This is why we make the effort to attend school and family reunions and root for our favorite sports teams; it is why we can become so passionately engaged in a cause we identify with or the community we live in.

One reason that experience with Dick Husselbee made such an impression is that his powerful sense of connection felt familiar to me. We've all felt a similar flood of memories about places and organizations we've been a part of. What would our world look like if all our leaders and managers were able to activate in others that sense of connection to their business, organization, campaign, or community? Wouldn't it make sense for *every* organization to strive to create this feeling in its members?

In fact, many organizations pour thousands and even millions of dollars each year into trying to increase employee engagement. In the United States alone, we spend more than $15 billion a year on leadership development programs. So why do so many people feel disconnected and disengaged from their workplace? The numbers are staggering: from 50 to 70 percent, according to a number of reliable studies. How well can these programs be working? Or is it that our leaders and managers are focusing on the wrong things?

This issue is a huge problem not only in the United States but around the world. As one study reported:

Disenchanted workers pull down productivity, increase churn, and darken the morale of the people around them. The annual economic costs are huge: as much as 100 billion Euros in France, US $64 billion in the UK, $6 billion in Singapore, and a whopping $350 billion in the United States. A crucial and often overlooked source of disengagement comes down to workplace relationships. Emerging research suggests that workplace toxicity may trump other factors when it comes to employee morale and performance. The first step in tackling workforce discontent may involve looking in the mirror. The

number one reason people leave comes down to *their relationship with their boss* [emphasis added].[1]

"As customers," observes productivity expert Terri Kabachnick,
"we've been waited on by people who quit but never left. As employees, we've been managed by bosses who quit but managed to
stay. As managers, we have managed people who physically attend
but mentally pretend."[2]

According to a 2010 survey by Right Management, a subsidiary
of the job-placement firm Manpower, about five in every six employees (84 percent) planned to seek a new position in 2011. Only
5 percent said they planned to stay in their current position.[3]

A recent Gallup poll showed that only 27 percent of US workers were "engaged" at work, while 69 percent were either "not engaged" or "actively disengaged."[4] Again, these figures reflect a
global reality. The study mentioned above showed that 80 percent
of British workers lack commitment to their jobs, with a quarter
being actively disengaged at work, and in France, only 12 percent
were actively engaged in their work. A Gallup poll of German
workers found that only 13 percent were actively engaged at work.[5]

---

1. Robin Athey, "It's 2008: Do You Know Where Your Talent Is?" Deloitte Devel-
    opment, 2004.

2. http://www.employeeretentionblog.com/employee-disengagement/
    disengagement-affects-everyone.

3. Press release, Right Management, December 13, 2010.

4. http://gmj.gallup.com/content/20770/gallup-study-feeling-good-matters-in-
    the.aspx.

5. http://gmj.gallup.com/content/117376/employee-disengagement-plagues-
    germany.aspx.

As powerful a force as genuine connection is, the *lack* of any real connection is an equally powerful force—only in the opposite direction. When you think about your workplace, can you identify people there who seem disengaged? Every one of us has friends, family, and acquaintances who have shared their stories of work disenchantment and disappointment. Sometimes this sense of disengagement can stem from something as seemingly minor as the thoughtless actions or attitudes of a single encounter.

Kristen, a young friend of mine, has worked for five years at a prestigious university in the community relations department. She was recently asked to prepare a briefing on a forthcoming event and to accompany the president in car rides to and from the event.

"I was so honored to have this assignment," she told me, "and very excited to meet our new president." Unfortunately, it did not prove to be a good experience. The president was dismissive and unpleasant to Kristen, treating her, as she put it, "as if I were invisible." Kristen confided to me that since that day, she has felt far less committed to her job. Chances are, this president was not even aware of the impact this experience had on Kristen, let alone its long-term negative consequences.

I remember a conversation with one of the administrative assistants in the development office at the Kennedy School in 2000 when I started there as director of Alumni and External Relations. She shared with me the fact that she had seven years, four months, and twelve days until her retirement. She was literally *counting the days* until she would no longer have to be there.

How many people are simply marking time in their jobs, waiting until the next three-day weekend, holiday, or vacation? Studies tell us it is at least five in every ten people.

Sometimes when people are unhappy at work, it's because

they're in an environment where they do not feel connected. They don't feel they belong there, that their contribution matters, or that they are valued as part of the team. When people don't feel connected, they disengage, tune out, or act out.

In a way, this is similar to how children feel sometimes. Why do children have tantrums? Often it's because they're frustrated that they don't have a voice, that they are not being heard, understood, or included. Adults have tantrums, too, and for the same reasons; we just do it in different ways. We may shut down in a meeting, or speak up aggressively, or join in the watercooler gossip and talk about people behind their backs, or treat them badly. We call in sick or spend the day on the Internet; we drink, overeat, rage, lie, or withdraw.

But it doesn't have to be this way, if we are willing to be conscious and recognize that engagement begins with the simple human desire to feel connected.

OUTSIDE THE GATES

In 1995, when I first took the position of director of the newly created White House Office for Women's Initiatives and Outreach (the Women's Office), one of the first key decisions facing us was where on White House property to physically locate our office. It came down to choosing between three very different options.

Option number one would be to situate the office on the ground floor of the West Wing together with the Office of Political Affairs. Although this would be a small desk space, without much room for staff or visitors, it would also be the most prestigious location of the three. In Washington, as in most any business or organization, access is typically viewed as power, and nothing suggests access like physical proximity.

The second option would be taking an office on the fifth floor in the Eisenhower Executive Office Building located directly next door to the West Wing—not nearly as prestigious as actually being *in* the West Wing, but still on White House property.

The third choice would be to set up our office across the street from the White House, in a row of government-owned town houses adjacent to Blair House and facing Lafayette Park. This property had three stories, with space for two conference rooms, a basement for supplies, and ample room for many staff, volunteers, and interns. It had charm, light, and space to grow.

In terms of Washington prestige and perception, this last option was clearly the worst of the three—but it was the best location for helping us achieve our mission, which was to create a connection with women's groups and women across the country who had historically not felt connected to their government.

The colorful and passionate Harold Ickes, deputy chief of staff, had set a clear mission for the office and empowered me to execute it. Harold always had my back; his support and involvement in the office were a significant part of its success.

We wanted the White House Women's Office to be a place where women in our government could connect with American women from all walks of life, as well as with each other. The "Townhouse" would allow us to create that atmosphere of accessibility, a place where women could drop by and feel welcome. We would have enough room to hold meetings of different sizes, and unlike being on site in the West Wing or the Eisenhower Executive Office Building, in this space visitors would be able to stop in without first having to be cleared by the Secret Service.

In many people's eyes, the Townhouse would be the *least* attractive choice. A West Wing location would be seen by some as a proud declaration of the importance of the Women's Office. But

being *effective* seemed to me the more important consideration. My
job was to build an effort that would educate, include, and advocate for women across the country. The Townhouse was the only
location that would really give us the space we needed to do so. So
I chose the Townhouse option—and never looked back.

The space turned out to be perfect. It allowed our tiny paid staff
to expand its productivity by providing room for ten volunteers
and ten interns, and still accommodated a constant stream of visitors every day. We kept the office supplied with a variety of baked
goods bought or donated by our team, creating a welcoming culture and sense of community that allowed guests to bring along
friends and colleagues without having to ask for permission. The
White House Women's Office also became a place of refuge for
women appointees throughout Washington, who would often stop
by the office after work. The space also allowed me to be physically
located together with my team.

The Townhouse gave us the opportunity to create the feel of a
genuine women's culture in a way that would have been impossible
in a more prestigious White House address. Our location may have
been "outside the gates" of *perceived* power, but it actually became
the source of our true power, which was the power to *connect*—
with our constituents, with our mission, and with each other.

STAYING CONNECTED TO REAL PEOPLE

Our choice of site for the Women's Office was a natural reflection of the way decisions were often made in the Clinton administration, because Bill and Hillary Clinton were keenly aware of
the power of connection, and the leader typically sets the tone of

the whole organization. In fact, one key aspect of President Clinton's leadership style was his desire to stay connected to everyday people and not become isolated. This is beautifully illustrated in a story Alexis Herman shared with me. Alexis served in the Clinton White House as head of Public Liaison and later as labor secretary.

It was in the early days of the president's first term; Alexis was about to hold her very first presidential briefing, and she was already nervous. The president had been delayed, and the minutes felt like hours as she waited for him to arrive in the East Wing. Finally he appeared with his personal aide, Andrew Friendly.

After apologizing for being so late, the president explained what had happened: Hillary was having a luncheon, and Andrew intended to make sure the president avoided the gathering so that he would stay on schedule. But instead of steering him away from the group, Andrew had inadvertently walked them right into the midst of it. When the elevator doors opened, there were all these people!

Andrew's face turned beet red. He was mortified.

"Oh, Mr. President," he said, "I'm so sorry! I didn't mean for you to stop here. I didn't mean for you to have to speak to all those people!"

And Clinton put his hand on his shoulder and said, "That's all right, Andrew, I used to be a people once myself."

After the president finished telling the group this story, he said, "When you work and live in the White House, with your own airplane and staff and all the trappings of the presidency, it's not easy to stay connected to real people."

He paused and then added, "If I have one goal for my presidency, that's it: to stay connected to real people. I expect over the years that will get harder and harder to do—but that's my goal."

A LAWYER'S HOMEWORK

The way we connect or don't connect with the people in our work-place can make a significant difference in progress on a project, in whether or not we are tapped for a promotion, or even in our over-all success. I heard a great example of this from Laureen Seeger, a very successful lawyer I met at a women's leadership conference.

Early in Laureen's career, when she first made partner at a major law firm, her colleagues told her, "Okay, now that you're a partner, you are responsible for bringing in new business. Go forth and build your client list!" So she applied herself and became quite a rainmaker, bringing in all kinds of business for the firm. She thought she was doing great, until a concern came up with a case she was working on—and she discovered that a senior partner had gone in and looked through her files.

She was completely taken aback. Why would he go into her files on his own, without telling her, instead of just coming to her and asking whatever he needed to know?

Many in this situation might just stew on it and feel resentful, defensive, or rattled. Laureen had the courage to take action. She called a meeting of the partners and asked them, "Is there a trust issue here? Is there something going on I don't know about?" In the course of the meeting they worked through the issue to some extent, but she still didn't feel resolved about why they hadn't simply come to her in the first place.

After the meeting, another partner who was also a friend took her aside. "The problem is," he said, "although you've brought a lot of business into the firm, you haven't gone about it in a way that's created any teamwork. You keep to yourself, you don't ask the other partners for help or tell anyone what you're doing.

There's a sense of being a little uncomfortable with you—because you haven't taken the time to get to know the people here."

They brainstormed about how to turn this misconception around, and came up with a simple plan: every day for the next three months, she would have lunch or coffee with one of the partners. That is exactly what she did, and as she built new relationships with her partners, their attitudes toward her shifted, which supported her growing success. Today she is executive vice president and general counsel for McKesson Corporation, the largest pharmaceutical distributor in the country.

The key point I took away from Laureen's story is that she was contributing at a high level *before* all this happened. What her experience shows is that you can be at the top of your game, doing an excellent job at your craft or profession—but no matter how good the work itself is, if you don't have good relationships with your colleagues, it may not have the impact or support it should.

How effective we are, at home and at work, depends on how fully and honestly we connect with other people. When we do, they become willing to participate and collaborate with us, not work against us. Our success is predicated to a great extent on how the people around us feel about us.

HOW TO BUILD RELATIONSHIPS

When speaking to women's groups and organizations, I'm often asked, "In an organization or company with a boys-club type of culture, how do you go about breaking in?"

The only answer I know is this: by building individual relationships. It ultimately comes down to the connections you create, one person at a time, and this applies equally to men and to breaking into *any* kind of organization or culture. Get to know people. Go out for coffee or grab a lunch. Talk.

Relationships create the alliances and collaborations it takes to get the work done. In any organization, those people who are the most successful over the long haul are the ones who have taken the time to build the necessary relationships.

This has certainly been true for me. The times in my life when I have been most successful were also times when my key relationships at work were solid. When those key relationships have not been as strong, or even lacking altogether, I have done less well or felt less confident about my results.

How do you go about creating those strong relationships? Over the years, many people have shared with me that they were not confident in their ability to approach someone they didn't know and build new business relationships, or that they simply felt they were not good conversationalists. I believe this is something anyone can learn, if they are curious about other people.

Engaging someone in conversation is about finding those things that might connect us, from knowing the same people to sharing similar interests. Conversations are opportunities to learn more about another person, share something about ourselves, and discover things we may have in common.

I had the opportunity to explore this idea not long ago with my daughter, Madison. Madison is someone who would consider herself shy with people she doesn't know, at least at first. "Mommy," she tells me, "I have gentle feelings."

One day after school she told me there was a boy at school she wanted to get to know, but she didn't know how to start a conversation with him. We started discussing how she might do this.

To begin with, I pointed out, most people like to talk about themselves.

"Ask him a question about *him*, or about something that interests him. How about asking him what he's doing for the summer? What camp is he going to, or what kind of vacation is his family taking? That shows him that you're curious about him and his life.

"And when you talk with him," I told her, "look him in the eyes. No one can engage with someone who's looking away. Looking at him shows that you value him and what he's saying.

"Finally, share something about yourself, too. When he tells you what he's doing this summer, then you can tell him what *you're* doing this summer."

Madison agreed that this sounded like a good plan and said she would try it the next day in the cafeteria at lunchtime. It worked; she was able to have a conversation with the boy, and since then she has continued practicing. She also shared this concept with her second-grade teacher, Erica Simons. Erica has introduced various cutting-edge ideas into her classroom. For example, she brought into her curriculum *The 7 Habits of Happy Kids*, by Sean Covey. Erica asked Madison if she would share these conversation-starting ideas with her classmates, and she did.

Imagine what the world would be like if we had all learned how to have meaningful conversations in grade school!

Simple as it seems, this works for adults as well. People know we are interested in them when we are curious enough to ask questions about them. At the same time, this is a two-way street. By sharing something relevant about ourselves, we pave the way for a genuine conversation. This is how we discover our common threads that become the basis for a connection.

It really boils down to two things: *curiosity* and *generosity*—the curiosity to ask questions about others and the generosity to share things about ourselves. Being curious about others and generous with ourselves is what allows us to make genuine connections.

THE STORY OF *US*

Building strong relationships within an organization not only fosters a stronger sense of connection and engagement, it also taps a powerful resource for getting things done.

This was exactly the organizing philosophy that Marshall Ganz shared with the staff and volunteer workers on the 2008 Obama campaign. It begins with the story of *oneself*, says Marshall, and that is the core of authenticity. But the process doesn't stop there. As Marshall puts it:

"The second story is the story of *us*. After developing our stories of self, the next step is to share those stories and, through those shared stories, to build relationships . . . and then you have the power to *act*."

This was something that showed up again and again as I began traveling to speak at Obama events in the fall of 2007. One of the first of these events took place in the crucial caucus state of Iowa, and it was there that I met Janet Petersen.

Janet is an attractive, personable young mom who serves as an Iowa state representative. During the months leading up to primary season, there was intense competition among the candidates to persuade state legislators to endorse them—especially in Iowa, given the state's pivotal position in the primary calendar. Janet was one of the very first legislators to endorse Senator Obama.

Janet was running for reelection for her fifth term in the Iowa

House, and she happened to be putting on a fund-raiser later on the same day as our Women for Obama (WFO) event. She had invited Senator Obama to attend, figuring it was a long shot. Much to her surprise, he accepted. She had also put in a request to have someone from the campaign join her in a roundtable conversation the following day with a group of mothers she had been working with. Their project had to do with helping prevent stillbirths and unexpected sudden infant death, and they hoped Senator Obama might be willing to support this work. Since I was planning to be in Iowa for the WFO event, the state staff added this meeting to my schedule.

When she heard the campaign chief operations officer would be coming, Janet expressed some hesitation. This was going to be a meeting about maternal health issues, not about the campaign or its operations, and it wouldn't be a very big group of people, just a small group of moms. She wasn't sure the COO was the right person to attend the meeting.

Her concern was understandable. The focus of this gathering was something quite personal to her: four years earlier, eight months into an apparently normal, healthy pregnancy, Janet and her husband, Brian, had lost their second baby, Grace Elizabeth. Of the half dozen women who would be getting together that day, every one of them had also lost a baby under very similar circumstances.

The campaign office assured Janet that with my history of working with women's issues, together with my dual role in the Obama campaign, I would be a perfect fit for this meeting. The date was set, and at shortly after noon on Sunday, October 14, the day after our WFO event and Janet's fund-raiser, I found myself gathered at lunch around a big round table at Biaggi's Ristorante Italiano in West Des Moines. Joining Janet and me around the table were Jan

Caruthers, Kerry Biondi-Morlan, Kate Safris, Betsy Burkhardt, and Amy McCoy. After Janet made the introductions, she shared the story of her pregnancy with Grace Elizabeth.

A BOND IN SHARED LOSS

Janet's due date was just before her son Charlie's second birthday. Everything about the pregnancy went perfectly: no morning sickness, just the right weight gain, all vital signs perfect—until week thirty-five.

"On Sunday night," Janet said, "a pain in the top part of my right leg was excruciating. I was up for a couple of hours before finally getting comfortable. I mentioned it to Brian and my mom the next morning. My mom suggested I call the doctor to make sure it wasn't anything serious."

The doctor had her come in that afternoon to be looked at. As the intake nurse examined her, she was puzzled to find she could not detect the baby's heartbeat. Another nurse tried, with no success. The doctor came in to do an ultrasound. He could not detect a heartbeat or any movement at all. Janet's completely normal, healthy baby had died.

"I delivered Grace Elizabeth the next day," Janet said. "She was a beautiful baby; she looked a lot like her big brother, Charlie. Five pounds, nine ounces, nineteen inches, a full head of hair—and a knotted umbilical cord that had cut off her blood supply."

After Janet's story, we continued around the table one by one, each of us sharing our own stories of loss. Their circle now included me as well, and not just as a visitor or observer—because a number of years before, I had lost a baby, too.

On December 8, 2000, our son, Parker, was born premature. While on a business trip, I had unexpectedly gone into labor, and at 23½ weeks, his lungs were not developed enough for him to survive. Dr. Obi, the wonderful obstetrician in attendance, did everything possible to stop the labor, but to no avail. I said hello and goodbye to my beautiful baby boy in a hospital in Houston, Texas.

Although my circumstances were slightly different from those of these other women, we all shared the same loss. For them, the losses had been more recent and the memories were still raw, while for me it had been almost seven years. Yet the fact that it was more distant in time didn't really make any difference. An experience like this is always a part of you, whether it happened months, years, or even decades ago.

As Marshall describes it, once we've established the connection that leads to "the story of us," that then leads to the next step, which is *action*. A shared sense of story brings out a shared sense of purpose, and it is from there that the force of a true movement is born.

This is exactly what had happened with Janet and the other women in the group, when they first began getting to know each other and finding that they had all had similar experiences. Their shared stories ignited in them all a desire to do something larger than themselves—to help other mothers avoid the same kinds of tragedies as they had suffered.

Speaking about the aftermath of her daughter's death, Janet said her doctors told her it was a fluke tragedy.

"It couldn't have been predicted or prevented, the doctors said. I was told this wasn't my fault, and that I'd have a better chance of winning the lottery than having it happen again."

But this was not accurate, as Janet and her friends learned in the course of their research. Grace Elizabeth's death was *not* a fluke, and it very likely could have been both predicted *and* prevented. As the women began meeting and sharing their experiences, they learned of a Louisiana obstetrician, Dr. Jason Collins, who had been studying umbilical cord accidents for more than fifteen years and had investigated hundreds of cases. According to Dr. Collins, these types of infant deaths are far more common than most people realize—and most could be avoided, if more people were aware of the warning signs.

For example, the American College of Obstetricians and Gyne-cologists (ACOG) recommends that you note the time it takes to feel ten kicks, jabs, turns, swishes, or rolls (not hiccups). By twenty-eight weeks, a healthy baby should have ten kicks in less than two hours. Most babies will take less than thirty minutes. A significant change in this pattern is one sign that there may be a problem. (For more information on these warning signs, go to www.countthekicks.org.)

"We were shocked to find that virtually nothing was being done to save the lives of the more than 26,000 babies who die of stillbirth causes in the United States every year," Janet said. "That's seventy babies per day!"

Janet and her friends started a prenatal health awareness move-ment dedicated to detecting early problems and avoiding these preventable tragedies. Sure enough, since helping get the word out to other women, they have heard from many mothers whose ba-bies' lives have been saved by the information they put out through their awareness campaign, Count the Kicks.[6]

I was touched by the courage and resilience of this small group of mothers, and was inspired to think about the number of lives

---

6. Janet and her team have also spearheaded legislative efforts, on both state and na-tional levels, to support this work. For more on the group and all they are doing, see www.countthekicks.org.

they had changed and would change through their shared wisdom and experience.

There is a bond that comes from the understanding and empathy of shared stories, and the connection we all formed that day continued throughout the campaign. Janet keeps me informed about their Count the Kicks campaign and we stay in touch to this day.

"WE CAME FOR BARACK, BUT WE STAYED FOR EACH OTHER"

Experiences like those in Marshall's storytelling sessions or Janet's lunch meeting at Biaggi's start out as very personal, but these are the moments that turn a story into a cause and a cause into a movement. And as Marshall often pointed out, they are sparked by the emotional connection of shared experiences.

Peachy Myers, a young woman who worked as a field organizer and then state field director for the Obama team (and who was one of my favorite people on the campaign trail), says it beautifully: "We came for Barack, but we stayed for each other." It is this sense of connection that leads people to take action.

People joined the campaign because they felt a connection to Barack Obama and his message. But it was the relationships they formed with each other on the ground that deepened and anchored that connection. The bonds they formed with one another were the glue that held this gigantic, growing grassroots organization together. People were passionately engaged from Portland, Maine, to Portland, Oregon, and it was this combination—their connection to the candidate along with the relationships forged with each other— that created the tidal wave of support that made a new president.

Organizations that appreciate and understand the power of connection can facilitate this kind of experience, often by simply fostering the kind of environment that allows it to happen naturally. In the Obama campaign, we made a decision early on to place most of our people with host families rather than in apartments or hotel rooms. This was in significant part a financial decision, because we wanted to conserve spending everywhere we could and make sure each dollar was spent with as much impact toward our goal as possible. But another reason was the closeness and sense of personal interaction it created between staff members and the local community.

A wonderful example of this is Elizabeth Vale. At the time, Elizabeth was one of the highest-ranking women at Morgan Stanley, where she served as managing director. Although she had never been involved in politics before, she became totally committed to the Obama campaign. Because we were committed to placing people with host families, Elizabeth opened her Pennsylvania home to staffers and volunteers, sometimes having as many as ten people at a time coming and going, using her kitchen and bathrooms at every hour of the day and night. There were hundreds of people like Elizabeth serving as host families all across the country.

After the election, Elizabeth went on to serve in the White House as President Obama's liaison to the business community and as executive director of the White House Business Council. In early 2011, she was appointed assistant director at the newly formed Consumer Financial Protection Bureau at the Treasury Department. She reports that she still stays in touch today with some of the people who came through her home during the course of the campaign.

Frank Brosens is another good example of how people inspired by the message and the candidate would join the campaign and then become fully engaged in the relationships and interactions formed at the grassroots level.

A very successful investment banker with Goldman Sachs for many years, Frank had taken time off to raise his five boys and chair a hospital board, and was now running a successful New York hedge fund. Like Elizabeth, Frank had never been at all politically active, but he was very impressed with Obama and felt he was the right leader for what needed to be done in the country.

Frank joined the campaign's national finance committee and spent the next year traveling from coast to coast to help the fundraising efforts. But his effort didn't stop there. He would show up at campaign offices and say, "Hey, what needs doing?" And whatever it was—stuffing envelopes, buying lunch for the staff, making phone calls to undecideds, walking neighborhoods and knocking on doors—he did it all without blinking an eye and loved every minute of it.

Another of my favorite examples of the power of connection is Kathleen Manning Hall. Married with three kids, Kathleen lives in Malden, Massachusetts, and works part-time doing administrative work in a law office as a legal assistant.

"I'm just a regular person," says Kathleen. "I was never involved in any political campaign before." But something changed in her when the United States invaded Iraq in 2003.

"I was very disillusioned with the state of the country at the time," Kathleen recalls. "At my oldest daughter's high school graduation, there was a boy graduating who had enlisted and was already on his way to Iraq, so his ten-year-old brother accepted his diploma for him. There was not a dry eye in the auditorium. I felt I had to do something. I had to get involved in some way."

When Kathleen heard Senator Obama's speech at the 2004 Democratic Convention, she was very inspired, and when he announced his candidacy in 2007, she began volunteering for the campaign. As she describes it, it became her personal mission to get him elected.

"I would wake up in the morning and ask myself, 'What can I do for the campaign today?'"

From that initial sense of passion and connection, Kathleen soon discovered strengths in herself she didn't know she had. She found that she enjoyed spending time talking with people about the campaign, especially people who, like herself, didn't really know much about politics.

"A lot of these people didn't think they could make a difference. But we would tell them, yes, they could make a difference—they *were* important, their votes *did* count and they *could* have a voice."

Kathleen also undertook coordinating the Massachusetts chapter of Women for Obama, working closely with its chair, Carol Fulp, planning fund-raisers and campaign trips to seven states. This was a new experience for someone who had never spoken in front of a group.

"It was an incredible feeling—the camaraderie with these women who shared the same commitment to this candidate and the same desire to change the country. It was a lot of work, but it was so satisfying. I would do it again in a heartbeat."

And she has. Today, with Kathleen's leadership, the Massachusetts chapter of Women for Obama has become New England Women for Change, a political action group supporting Democratic candidates throughout the country.

PEOPLE, CONNECTION, AND TECHNOLOGY

It was during my time working on the campaign at our Chicago headquarters that I began to experience what an impact technology has had on how people communicate with each other—for better and for worse.

On the macro level, technology had a profoundly positive impact on the campaign, and the team's innovative use of these new tools played a big role in our ultimate success. Within the team itself, however, technology sometimes seemed to me to create more separation than connection. At HQ, staff would often walk down the halls with their eyes glued to their Black-Berrys, and the campaign office (like most offices today) was a sea of faces staring at their computer screens. When someone sitting nearby wanted your response to something, it was more the norm that he would email you than phone you or poke his head in your office door.

This is the way we've come to operate, and it has brought with it all kinds of gains in productivity—but a strength taken to an extreme can become a weakness. Today we find ourselves having a national conversation about how much is too much, what are the limits of multitasking, and what we may be giving up in the name of "efficiency." Increasingly, in the home as well as the workplace, we are wondering to what extent our dedication to our gadgets is causing us to disconnect from each other.

People often ask me about how technology affects our sense of connection. It's not a simple answer.

The truth is, *leaders use technology*. In fact, this is one of the hallmarks of leadership: effective leaders make sure they are staying on top of how the world is changing, and new technologies for communication are often at the top of the list. The Obama campaign became famous for its intelligent and insightful use of the Internet and social media, and it was certainly a pivotal factor in its success. But interestingly, much of our social media strategy actually focused on using technology to drive *more* face-to-face interactions, from opportunities to volunteer in the offices to attendance at house parties, town halls, and rallies.

It's important not to see technology as something that can replace live, in-person contact. Email, text messaging, Facebook, and all the other digital means of staying in touch are incredibly convenient and powerful. But does having 2,000 friends on Facebook really mean you are engaging in 2,000 meaningful friendships?

A friend of mine tells me that in her company, they now do all their team interaction online, with no more face-to-face meetings. "I don't even know my colleagues," she says, adding that she now feels completely disconnected from her workplace.

Technology allows us to be highly efficient. But again, in any organization, our success is ultimately predicated on how the people around us feel about us. Our goal as leaders is to have an empowered, engaged team. No matter what our job description might be, cultivating relationships and connection is a hugely important part of our work.

INTEGRATION BREAKFASTS

When I began working at the Chicago headquarters we went from 30 to 300 people virtually overnight, and many of us didn't know each other. After a few months, I began holding weekly gatherings in my office that we called *integration breakfasts.*

For the next few months, ten different staff members from each department of the campaign would come together for breakfast each week. We would start off with each of us sharing a bit about our background and why we chose to join the campaign. Each staff member would describe what was happening in their area of the campaign, and we would then open up the discussion about what was going right in the campaign's operations and what could be improved.

I wouldn't say these breakfasts had a dramatic impact on the course of the campaign, but they made a quiet difference. People got to connect with each other in a more personal way and build new relationships across the campaign. If they needed something in another department, now there was a better chance that they would actually know the person they were calling. These informal get-togethers also helped me get to know our campaign staff on a more personal basis, and they got to learn more about their COO. What's more, I got to hear input directly from staff members in a way that no memos or conference calls, email blasts or intranets could duplicate.

It doesn't take a major corporate policy decision or top-down mandate to create an informal forum like this. It's so simple and easy to do. And whether in a corporate office, a nonprofit organization, a school or university, or any other kind of environment, it can do wonders for the organization's overall sense of morale, cohesion, and common purpose. You can create this kind of opportunity for relationship-building in any organization and on any scale—as I saw during my time at the Clinton White House Women's Office, when we created a program to reach out and connect with everyday women across the country. We called it *At the Table*.

AT THE TABLE

To share how At the Table came to be, I first have to explain what it feels like to work at an agency in the federal government.

There are more than 150,000 federal employees in Washington, DC. Of these, 3,000 are appointed by the president to carry out the administration's agenda; they are referred to as *political appointees*. Working as a political appointee in our nation's capital can be very exciting, but it can also feel like you are an anonymous drop of water in a very large ocean. You may work only blocks from the White House, but it can seem like you're on the other side of the universe. Most political appointees are devoted public servants who work long hours, with no job security, to serve their country. Yet many rarely (or never) have the opportunity to interact with the heads of their own agencies, let alone the president. It's easy to start feeling disconnected and lose sight of the passion that brought you there.

In 1995, during my first few months working at the White House, I made it a priority to visit all the top federal agencies and meet with the women appointees to let them know that the new White House Women's Office was a resource for them.

"We are your connection to the White House," I told them, "and we want to hear from you. What are you working on that the president should know about?"

We began hosting monthly programs for the women political appointees both at the White House and at the federal agencies. A cabinet secretary would volunteer to host an evening, we would bring in a well-known speaker, and a few hundred appointees would attend from across the agencies. At one event to celebrate Women's History Month, we had Gloria Steinem and Evelyn Lieberman speak (Evelyn was the first woman to serve as White House deputy chief of staff and an important mentor for me)—and about 900 appointees showed up!

Soon we came up with an idea that would eventually take on a life of its own. The idea grew out of a family story about my sister JoJo, who forgot to vote in the 1992 election. This was particularly egregious to our sister Dee Dee, who had worked as Governor Clinton's press secretary during his presidential campaign that year. But JoJo was far from alone; in fact, given the opportunity to cast their votes in the 1992 election, 54 million Americans passed. Even today, millions of intelligent, informed, committed, active people don't vote. Why not? Because many people don't feel their vote really matters, or don't feel connected to their government.

We wanted to find a way to reach all those women who were not already involved in women's advocacy groups and would not normally feel much connection to politics or Washington. We brainstormed about different ways we might do that.

One day that fall, Judy Gold, our Women's Office policy director, exclaimed, "I got it! We all have a JoJo in our lives, friends and family back home who don't feel connected. We're all going home at Thanksgiving, right? What a perfect time to sit at the table with our families and find out what's on their minds. What would they want the president to know? We could call it At the Table."

We all agreed that it was a brilliant idea—and so simple! At the Table was launched over that Thanksgiving holiday with fifty roundtable discussions hosted by our women appointees in communities across the nation. We invited the appointees' hometown newspapers to attend, many of whom took us up on the invitation. That weekend generated a flurry of stories across the country with headlines like HOME-TOWN GIRL COMES HOME ON BEHALF OF THE PRESIDENT, with each article including pictures and stories about that appointee and her contribution to the administration.

The program created quite a buzz, and we kept doing these

events. In time things snowballed, and over the following year we organized and held roughly 1,500 of these intimate gatherings. We collected and collated all the feedback from the women at all the events, and every quarter we compiled a report and delivered it to the president, who got to hear what real people out in the cities and towns were thinking.

The president was intrigued with the program and agreed to do one himself. And so it was that on July 21, 1996, Mary Frances Kelley's nine-year-old daughter Christina greeted President Bill Clinton at the front door of their home on Magnolia Way in Denver, Colorado. "Thank you for having me in your home," said the president, and for the next ninety minutes, Mary Kelley and fifteen other women sat around her living room with the president of the United States, sipping iced tea while they discussed everything from day care to gang violence, preventive health care to the environment, domestic violence to age discrimination.

The president told the gathering (echoing his earlier remarks to Alexis) that one of the most difficult things about being president is managing to stay in regular contact with the nation's citizens, and that he was eager to hear what they had to say.

"He listened a good deal more than he talked," recalls Mary, a single mom and successful entrepreneur, "and he asked really good questions. We could tell they weren't scripted or prepared, because they grew out of what each person had just said. I think everyone came away from the conversation with some new ideas and a better connection to our government and our president."

The last few years of President Clinton's presidency were very difficult, yet he survived them because of the reservoir of goodwill he had built up over the years. When he left the White House in 2001 he had an approval rating of *66 percent*—the highest of any departing US president since World War II. How was that possible? Because of the sense of personal connection he creates with people.

A LASTING IMPACT

The impact of those At the Table events is still being felt today, more than fifteen years later, as I learned from my friend Anne Reed. Anne worked in the Clinton administration in a senior position at the Department of Agriculture, and she hosted many of these events.

"I thought it was an absolutely wonderful idea," Anne says, "so I did as many of these gatherings as possible, and each time, I came back wanting to do more. It was just an amazing thing to sit in someone's living room, or a small restaurant meeting room, or an office at a law firm, and be surrounded by women who were completely blown away by the notion that the president of the United States was genuinely interested in what they had to say.

"It had a major impact on their lives, because they really did feel they were being listened to. And it was a reminder for us, the political appointees, that we served and represented the president, and it made us feel proud. Yet it was so simple, so easy to do, and it cost absolutely nothing but a little time."

Anne led one of these At the Table events at her mother's home in Nashville. In her late seventies at the time, Anne's mother invited over a number of friends her own age, many of whom Anne had known when she was a young girl.

"They came because my mother asked," Anne recalls, "but also because they were genuinely intrigued. Many were wives of doctors, university professors, and other professionals, and most were

extremely well educated—but like other women of their generation, they did not have jobs outside the home. They were very
aware politically but not politically active. They definitely crossed
party lines. And to a person, they were able to engage in substan-
tive conversation and debate about issues."

Over the years after serving in the Clinton White House, Anne
and I continued to stay in touch. We caught up over lunch recently,
and in the course of our conversation she shared that her mother
had recently passed away. At the funeral she saw many of her
mother's longtime friends—and to her amazement, they all talked
about that event they had attended in Anne's mother's living room
more than a decade earlier.

"Some of these women shared how much that event meant to
them," she told me. "They'd felt they had a voice that was going
to be heard—and they had never felt that way before. In fact, they
said, it was one of the highlights of their lives."

She paused, then added, "We walk through so many other people's lives and often don't know the lasting impact we have."

Just as with Dick Husselbee, it didn't matter how many years
had passed: the connection was still there.

How to Take the Lead

Feeling connected to others is what gives our lives meaning and
fuels our sense of belonging. That sense of connection speaks to
our desire to identify with and feel part of something bigger than
ourselves, and leads us to take action.

- Do you take the time to really get to know the people you work
  with? No matter how good your work is, if you don't build good

relationships with your colleagues, it may not have the impact and support it could.

- How effective you are, at home and at work, depends on how fully and honestly you connect with other people. Go out for coffee or grab a lunch. Find opportunities to spend a little free time just talking.

- Are you comfortable starting conversations with people you don't know yet? Remember that conversations are opportunities to discover things we share in common. The two keys to genuine conversation are the *curiosity* to ask questions about the other person and the *generosity* to share something about yourself.

- Remember that building strong relationships within an organization not only fosters a stronger sense of connection and engagement, it also taps a powerful resource for getting things done. The story of *us* gives us the power to *act*.

- In your organization, look for opportunities for people to meet informally, share personal stories, and build relationships. The emotional connection of shared experiences creates moments that turn a story into a cause, and a cause into a movement.

- What role do social media and other new technologies play in your work? Do you use these technologies to help bring people together, or keep them apart? Look for ways to use new social media tools to drive *more* face-to-face interaction rather than less.

3. RESPECT

Seeing Past the Sunglasses

In October 1995, the Clinton White House held an event in observance of National Domestic Violence Awareness Month. This was an issue President Clinton deeply cared about and one where he made substantial progress during his presidency. Partnering with the private sector, he was announcing some key initiatives for domestic violence awareness in the workplace. Among the roughly two hundred guests in attendance were a number of prominent members of the business community, top executives of major corporations who were advocates and champions of this cause. Jerry Rossi, president of the Marshalls chain of department stores, had been chosen to represent them.

"I was going to work one morning, a few years ago," Jerry began in his remarks to the assembled guests and press in the East Room. "I walked into the elevator at our building, on the way up to my office. There was just one other person in the elevator with me, a young woman with her head down.

"It was the middle of winter," he added, "and dark outside— and she was wearing sunglasses."

Jerry didn't know this woman personally; she was one of roughly 1,400 Marshalls associates working in the building. But the way she kept turning away from him made Jerry keenly aware that something was not right. He introduced himself and asked her if she would take a few minutes to have a cup of coffee.

"Once we were upstairs sitting down to coffee," Jerry told the East Room audience, "I said, 'Why don't you take off your sunglasses? You don't need them in here.'"

The woman said she would prefer to leave them on, if that was all right.

Jerry gently asked her, "Is there something you want to talk about?"—and she started to cry. She did take her sunglasses off then, and Jerry saw that she had not one but two black eyes.

"My husband said if I told anyone," she confessed, "then he would *really* hurt me." She was afraid for herself, and even more afraid for their two young children.

Within two weeks Jerry managed to get a restraining order against the woman's husband and find a new living situation for her and her children. Just to make sure she was safe, he also had people from the company's security department escort her to her car every night after work for the next several months.

Throughout her ordeal, she was supported by Jerry and his staff to get back on her feet, and today, more than fifteen years later, she is still with the company. Her life and the lives of her children have been profoundly changed for the better—and all because Jerry took the time to recognize that there was a *person* behind the sunglasses.

MAKING THE EFFORT TO NOTICE

As the top executive of a national retail firm, it was Jerry's responsibility to direct the operation of all their hundreds of stores and ensure that their stockholders saw a profit. One might think that looking out for the personal welfare of one associate among the 1,400 who worked in his building was not, strictly speaking, part of his job description.

Except that, to Jerry, *it was.*

Someone else in the elevator that day might have chosen to avoid the uncomfortable situation, or not have even noticed the unusual behavior in the first place. For many, it would have been easier to just walk out of the elevator and on to the day's busy schedule, or perhaps to extend this one woman a brief helping hand (or delegate the task to someone in Human Resources) and then let that be that. But not for Jerry.

In fact, helping this one woman and her family was only the beginning. This event became part of an awakening for Jerry. He soon became aware that the woman he had met in the elevator was not the only person in his company dealing with this problem.

"The more I learned about how widespread this kind of situation was," Jerry told me recently, "the more outraged I got."

He went on to make domestic violence awareness a mission at the TJX Companies (owners of Marshalls) and throughout the nation.[1] To Jerry, this went beyond "handling an employee issue"—it became a *cause.* A founding father of the nonprofit Family Violence Prevention Fund, Jerry has become a national spokesman for the cause, traversing the country to speak to audiences at corporations, health-care organizations, and colleges. "I am a traveling cold shower for the business community," he says. "I tell them, this problem is out there, it's real, and we need to do something about it."

---

1. Later that year, Marshalls was purchased by TJX; today, Jerry is group president of the TJX Companies.

For Jerry, this sense of awareness is not limited to the work he has done around this particular issue. This is how he approaches everyone in his business and in his life. Jerry operates from a philosophy that says *people matter,* and that goes to the heart of what so moved me about the event that October day in the East Room. He embodied what to me is the essence of real leadership. It's about opening your eyes and seeing the people around you, taking the time to talk with them and become conscious of what's going on in their lives.

This is more than just a nice way of being; it also has a powerful impact on the bottom line. The TJX Companies is a multibillion-dollar Fortune 500 company, one of the most successful apparel chains in the world. Jerry's kind of leadership gets *results.*

"When I first got involved in the issue of domestic violence," says Jerry today, "most towns in the United States wouldn't even send a [police] cruiser to answer a domestic violence call. They considered it a 'private thing.' And when cases did make it to court, many judges would dismiss them without even hearing them. Not anymore. Today the law enforcement agencies and judicial system are behind this 110 percent."

President Clinton's commitment to this issue had much to do with this progress. He is the only American president so far to have made domestic violence, a problem that affects one in four American women and is the number one killer of women worldwide, a top priority of his administration.

In his own remarks that day, President Clinton closed with words I will never forget:

> Let me say to all the women here and all across America who are abused or who have been abused, you are not invisible.

These people have stood with you today, and you can now know that you are being heard, you are being seen, you are being understood.

GOVERNING BY LISTENING

In the spring of 2010, I traveled to Taiwan to speak at two leadership forums. During this visit I had the chance to spend some time with the governor of Taipei County, Hsi-Wei "Joe" Chou, who was hosting one of the events.

On the day of our forum, as Governor Chou and I walked together through the Taipei County government building on our way to the event, we suddenly heard shouting and saw a scuffle some distance off. As we got closer we saw what the commotion was about: four security guards were struggling to apprehend a distraught man who was frantically waving a piece of paper in the air and screaming that he wanted to speak with the governor. The paper, as we soon learned, was a letter this man had written to Governor Chou about an indignity that he claimed had happened to him. He was insisting that he be allowed to deliver the letter in person.

The security guards, conscious that the governor would soon be passing by with guests, seemed especially anxious to contain the man. However, rather than simply walking past and avoiding the uncomfortable situation, Governor Chou approached the man and asked the guards to please back away and give them some space to talk together.

Addressing the man quietly and directly, the governor was able to calm the situation quickly. He promised to read the man's letter and look into the situation personally.

"It is about treating people with respect and showing them you care," he said to me as we continued walking. "Whether the man is right or wrong, or even if he has mental issues, he deserves the respect of his government and his governor."

This small impromptu act revealed more about how Hsi-Wei Chou governs than any prepared remarks on the public panel that day could have possibly conveyed. Whether or not the man's grievance was justified, the governor understood instinctively that he deserved to be heard.

People want to feel that their voice matters. Effective leaders understand this and take the time and care to listen and make sure people feel truly heard. This goes beyond being a "leadership strategy" or conscious means to an end. Leaders listen to people because it's simply who they *are*.

LETTING OTHERS HAVE THEIR VOICE

Respect means being willing to listen and let others have their voice, even when it might be inconvenient, difficult, or painful to do so. This doesn't mean we have to agree with another's decision or opinion. It simply means being willing to listen and appreciate people for their unique perspective. In fact, it is usually when we *don't* agree with what other people are saying that listening is especially important—and especially powerful.

A striking example of this occurred in the midst of a very challenging time in the summer of 1996, near the end of President Clinton's first term.

It was just one week before the Democratic Convention in Chicago, heading into the heart of reelection season. In three days, the president planned to sign a controversial piece of legislation:

the Personal Responsibility and Work Opportunity Reconciliation Act. In two words, *welfare reform*.

Welfare reform was something President Clinton had been committed to for a long time, even long before he was president. He believed in his head and heart that the current welfare system stripped people of their self-esteem, and that reforming the system was not only a financially important goal but also a fundamental act of respect for the people involved. He believed that increased self-sufficiency would mean increased self-worth, and that the next generation would benefit tremendously from having been raised by working parents. In his first State of the Union address, he promised to "end welfare as we know it . . . to make welfare a second chance, not a way of life, exactly the change most welfare recipients want it to be." He was now intent on making good on that promise.

The reforms he wanted to enact were sweeping, especially the addition of work requirements and time limits: under the proposed new regulations, after two consecutive years of being on the welfare rolls, one would need to go to work, and there would be a lifetime cumulative limit of five years on welfare per individual.

Not surprisingly, his effort met with a huge wave of opposition and backlash. This was legislation that went back to FDR, sixty years of established legislative history he wanted to change, and it wasn't going to happen without a lot of compromise on both sides of the political spectrum. There was general consensus among Democrats and Republicans that we needed to pass some kind of welfare reform. But conservatives thought some provisions were too generous, and liberals saw others as too harsh. The president had already vetoed two versions of the bill; a third version now sat on his desk. On August 1, he announced that he would soon sign this third version of the bill.

Shock and disappointment reverberated throughout the traditional Democratic groups. Although the president repeatedly
stated his intention to revisit and improve the bill after its passage,
through both congressional and non-congressional means, this did
little to quell the wave of outrage washing over us in the White
House.

This had shaped up as *the* hot issue in the days leading up to the
convention. Threats of floor demonstrations inside the convention
hall had all of us who oversaw different constituencies extremely
worried. Some constituents went on hunger strikes, others pick-
eted in front of the White House, and still others demanded resig-
nations of White House and agency staff who had failed to change
the president's mind—myself included.

One person who believed strongly that we had to keep the process moving, no matter how polarized the situation, was Alexis
Herman, the White House director of the Office of Public Liaison.

In the White House hierarchy, director of Public Liaison is a key
senior position.[2] This is the person who manages communication
with all the demographic and interest groups usually referred to
as *constituencies,* including women's groups, the African-American
community, the Hispanic community, various faith-based groups,
gay and lesbian groups, business, the disabled, and many others.
The Office of Public Liaison invites representatives of all such
groups to the White House to convey the president's position on
different issues and gain their support. In her capacity as Public Liaison director, Alexis was truly on the front lines.

Alexis is a beautiful, elegant woman with the graciousness of

---

2. In May 2009, the Office of Public Liaison was renamed the Office of Public
Engagement.

a diplomat. She is also passionate about improving the lives of women, children, and families living in poverty.

"I started life as a social worker," says Alexis, "and I was very aware that women don't really *want* to be on welfare; they want to work, they want to take care of their children and provide for their families. But there's a lot of historical pain associated with being on welfare. It wasn't just the moment we had to break through, it was all that historical pain and long-term demonization of the issue."

We decided to invite the national leaders of the women's groups to the White House to keep the dialogue open and reiterate the president's desire to work with the constituencies to improve the bill. Even once it was signed, there would still be ample opportunity—for example, through the drafting of regulations and working with the individual states—to determine exactly how it would be implemented on a state and local level. These women leaders knew these issues inside and out, and their input and participation would be crucial to ensure that we ended up with the best results possible.

So, on August 19, the president's fiftieth birthday—and just three days before he was to sign the bill—Alexis and I hosted a listening session in the White House Women's Office. The meeting lasted almost two hours.

"THE BEST MEETING I EVER ATTENDED"

Alexis started the session off with a few brief remarks. "Thank you for your willingness to come here today," she said to the women who had assembled there. "We know you're upset. We know the bill isn't perfect, and we want you to know that the president is committed to improving it. Please don't abandon us—we need your help to get this done."

She looked around the room and said, "Today is about listening and hearing from you." Then she opened up the floor—and for the next hour and fifty-five minutes we said next to nothing. We simply listened.

The women felt frustrated, defeated, and even worse, betrayed. To them this was a huge setback for their life's work toward improving the lives of poor women and children. They believed this bill would actually hurt the very people the president intended to help.

We let them know we sympathized, without judgment or trying to convince them of our viewpoint. We didn't dismiss them, argue with them, disagree, or agree—we simply listened.

The meeting finally broke up and, one by one, the women leaders left the office. Alexis and I looked at each other blearily. It had felt like a very unproductive meeting, and we were both completely drained.

The next morning, our office started receiving feedback from the women who had attended the listening session. As my team shared the phone messages, I stopped in my tracks. One after the other, they were all similar—and they were all extremely positive!

"Thanks so much for inviting us in to talk," said one woman leader, "for being so open to dialogue and respecting what we had to say." Another said, "That was the best White House meeting I've ever attended."

I repeated it to myself over and over: *That was the best White House meeting I've ever attended.*

I was stunned. To us, it had felt like a painful and unsuccessful meeting—but to her, it had felt positive and productive! Where we had interpreted the level of discontent as a sign that we made little progress together, these women had a very different experience—because they felt *heard*.

I'll never forget the lesson I learned that day: sometimes the only way to keep the process going is to listen, no matter how difficult the issue seems or how stalled it has become. We hadn't necessarily solved anything that day, but we had kept the process going.

TRUST WORKS

How people handle conflict and disagreement tells you a lot about them. Some meet conflict head-on with aggression and confrontation, which often only exacerbates the problem. Some ignore it or seek to avoid it altogether, while others try to soften conflict by telling everyone what they want to hear, or by avoiding telling all the facts. But no matter what the conflict is, keeping everyone in the room and the process going depends on whether or not we are able to establish trust.

Here is how Alexis put it:

"When people don't trust you, you really do have to go the extra mile. You have to listen and *gain* their trust before you can even *have* a conversation. That session was not about trying to win agreement. It was about winning trust. Because you can disagree honorably once you have a trust relationship."

The following week at the convention in Chicago, we held similar meetings with Secretary of Health and Human Services Donna Shalala, whose agency would oversee much of the work on the welfare reform bill's regulations. As in our White House meeting, we spent that time listening to the ideas of the women leaders who had spent their entire careers on these issues.

The women we met with hadn't changed their minds when they left those meetings. They still disagreed with the president, but they did not abandon us, and there were no floor demonstrations at the convention. We managed to keep the dialogue open, and during the next few years, in partnership with the women's community, we *were* able to make some significant improvements in the bill's impact. (As just one example, working with the Department of Health and Human Services, we were able to help create regulations in many states that provided for the extension of time limits on welfare benefits for women who were victims of domestic violence.)

The impact welfare reform had ultimately proved to be enormous, both socially and economically. Over the following ten years welfare rolls dropped from 12.2 million to 4.5 million. Sixty percent of the mothers who left welfare found work, far surpassing many experts' predictions. Through the Welfare to Work Partnership, which began during President Clinton's second term under the leadership of Eli Segal, more than 20,000 businesses hired more than one million former welfare recipients.[3]

ARE YOU BEING TUNED OUT?

In my role as director of the White House Women's Office, I was part of the senior staff meetings held every morning in the Roosevelt Room with White House chief of staff Leon Panetta. Each

---

3. Bill Clinton, "How We Ended Welfare, Together," *New York Times*, August 22, 2006.

meeting began with a rundown of the president's schedule and the important issues of the day, and then each staff member would have the opportunity to report on any pressing issues or concerns from his or her portfolio.

Rahm Emanuel, who would later serve as President Obama's chief of staff before going on to become mayor of Chicago, was a colleague at the time. Our portfolios overlapped: Rahm's covered crime and mine was focused on women, so we interacted on such areas as domestic violence, deadbeat dads, and abortion-clinic bombings. One day Rahm pulled me aside.

"Betsy," he said, "can I make a suggestion about how you're presenting your issues and topics in the morning meeting?"

"Sure," I replied, "tell me."

He went on to say that I sounded more like one of the women advocates pushing from the outside than a member of the president's staff working on the inside.

"We're tuning you out," he explained. "You need to tell us why something is important for the president, not just because it is what the women's groups want."

I'd had no idea this was how I was being perceived, and this was one of those "Aha" moments for me. Fortunately, it was still early enough in my White House tenure that I was able to make a course correction and reframe how I presented these issues. I was grateful to Rahm for his honesty and willingness to tell me the truth. (If you know Rahm or have read much about him, you can probably appreciate that I've told a kinder, gentler version of the story, and that this wasn't quite the actual language he used. Either way, I got the message.)

Several years later I mentioned this conversation to Rahm, and he didn't remember giving me this advice—yet for me it was a meaningful insight from a colleague I respected, and it was very helpful to me. Sometimes sharing a simple observation or bit of feedback with a colleague can be tremendously valuable to them. In this case, Rahm's observation led me to think more broadly about how I was communicating, whether I found myself in the Oval Office with the president or in any meeting with constituents, colleagues, or my own staff.

The way we communicate and frame an issue, and our awareness of the timing and context, can make all the difference in how we are heard (or even whether we are heard at all!) and what results we get. If we have five minutes with someone and several issues to discuss, which are most important to bring up right now? What is the best way to frame an issue based on that person's interest, knowledge of the issue, and competing demands? Given what else that person has on his or her plate, is this the best time for us to bring this issue up?

In other words, a key part of how effective we are in our communication is the respect we show for our intended audience in the way we frame that communication in the first place.

ARE YOU THE RIGHT PERSON TO VOICE THE INITIATIVE?

Sometimes, in order to make sure your idea is heard, it is necessary to ask yourself whether you are the best person available to communicate. Who is the right person, with the right position, credibility, or relationships, to help move your idea, program, or initiative forward?

I first realized this in 1994, when I served on the Interagency Committee on Women's Business Enterprise. Congress had passed legislation requiring that this committee include one person from every government agency to represent and champion opportunities for women small-business owners. Most of the committee appointments were high-ranking women from each agency; for example, Laura D'Andrea Tyson, chair of the president's Council of Economic Advisers, had been appointed as committee chair.

I invited John Deutch, then deputy secretary of defense, to be part of our committee, and he graciously agreed. The defense department gives millions of dollars in federal contracts to small-business owners; a portion of those contracts go to women business owners. John's involvement on the committee would send a signal that this issue was not only important but important enough for the deputy secretary of defense to get involved.

We held a meeting at the White House where Deutch spoke, and, sure enough, his position, along with the fact that he was a man saying how important this issue was, gave our committee and mission increased credibility. I will always be grateful to him.

I saw this again at the Center for Public Leadership in 2005, when I had the idea of bringing to Harvard a cutting-edge leadership program called the Hoffman Process.

Based in California's Napa Valley, the Hoffman Process is an eight-day program that focuses on our patterns of behavior, learned from childhood, that often keep us from being our authentic selves and achieving the happiness we are capable of. I had attended the program in the fall of 2003 and believed that Kennedy School graduate students would benefit tremendously from this experience.

At the same time, it was far enough outside the mainstream of traditional Ivy League educational programs that whoever sold this idea successfully to the school's leadership would have to make a compelling case—and I realized that I might not be the right person to make that case. Considering who might be the best messenger for the task, I thought of Steve Belkin.

Founder of Trans National Group Services, Steve is a very successful Boston business owner and Harvard Business School alumnus. He was on the board of the Hoffman Institute and very open about the difference the program had made in his life.

Given Steve's stellar reputation in the Boston business community, as well as his Harvard Business School pedigree and Boy Scout good looks, I believed our dean would be better able to hear about the program from Steve than from me.

Steve and I discussed the idea and decided to frame it as a pilot program, to be held over spring break at an off-campus location. Steve then spent some time discussing the idea with David Gergen and our colleagues at the center, and also with the Kennedy School's dean, David Ellwood. Both Gergen and Dean Ellwood agreed to the plan, and we were able to move forward. The program ran successfully for four years, with more than 150 graduate students participating.

Although I knew the program well and had the passion and ability to sell it, in this context I was not the best person to advocate for it. Steve had more in common with the decision makers and was better positioned to give the idea its best representation.

At a Washington, DC, law firm I recently met a woman who is responsible for the firm's diversity efforts. She shared with me how far many law firms still have to go in their efforts to support advancement for women and minorities. "Many firms talk the talk," she said, "but don't have the infrastructure to do what needs doing on this issue—or the depth of commitment."

A partner with the firm and also an African-American, she nonetheless had not been able to get her partners' full attention on this issue. She shared with me the strategy she had planned.

First, she identified some of the firm's biggest and most profitable clients who also believed that diversity and inclusion were a key factor in their choice of law firm. Then, she formed a committee around this issue that included some of these same clients.

Suddenly, the senior partners were willing to look at the issue and give it the time and resources it needed and deserved.

It's not about ego, and it's not about who had the idea in the first place: it's thinking strategically about who is the best person to get the job done.

A MAJOR HURDLE

In early January 2007, when I was still trying to decide whether to leave the Center for Public Leadership and join the newly forming Obama presidential campaign staff as COO, I had a meeting with Senator Obama at his office on Capitol Hill.

"I still haven't made my final decision about whether I'm running," he said, "but I will in the next day or so, and if I do enter the race, I want to run a different kind of campaign."

Different in what way, I asked.

"For starters," he said, "I want to run a campaign that is inclusive, that makes it easy for people to participate and get involved. That also means having a well-run, disciplined organization. And the other thing is, I want to run a campaign that is about *respect*. One that respects our staff, our volunteers, our donors, and especially the voters."

You don't hear *that* very often in political campaigns. In a political campaign there is typically one objective: get your candidate elected—and there's no time for *please* or *thank you*. But Obama's vision was different. His campaign would be one that created a culture of inclusion across the country.

As the campaign played out over the following months, it did largely stay true to that vision, and the senator himself embodied this ideal of respect, staying out of the fray of negative campaigning, nasty altercations, and sparring matches that are so typically part of the campaign process. Still, as strongly as the Obama campaign reflected the value of respect, it was not without its flaws. There was one critical issue that the campaign misdiagnosed, and that was how deep the feelings ran among Hillary Clinton's supporters, and how difficult it would be for them to let go of their dream once it became clear that Obama, and not Clinton, would be the Democratic nominee.

Starting from the Iowa caucus on January 3, 2008, and lasting clear through the primaries of Montana, South Dakota, and Puerto Rico in the first week of June, the Democratic primary contest proved to be far more prolonged than anyone anticipated. Everyone—the voters, the media, the campaign teams themselves—was looking for a clear signal that one candidate had the clear upper hand. But in contest after contest, it kept looking like a dead heat.

In the aftermath of that long and difficult primary season, a whole new challenge appeared. There were now hundreds of thousands of Hillary supporters who were deeply disappointed. Many were angry—and many were quite ambivalent about their support for Senator Obama. In fact, "ambivalent" is putting it mildly: a substantial number of Hillary supporters were actually talking about supporting John McCain!

Winning the party's nomination was one thing. Winning the trust and hearts of these huge numbers of grieving Hillary supporters now became a significant hurdle.

Suddenly I started getting calls from women I'd known during my time in the Clinton administration, asking if I was available to meet with some of the Hillary supporters. I hadn't known anyone on the staff when I joined the Obama campaign, and these women were now in the same boat: for many of them, I was the only person they knew from the Obama campaign. This became my most focused and personal responsibility at this point in the campaign. And this is when I began to fully appreciate some sound advice David Gergen had shared with me eighteen months earlier.

"MAKE SURE YOU LET PEOPLE KNOW"

After meeting with Senator Obama back in early January 2007, I needed some outside perspective, so I went to see David Gergen. Millions of people know and trust David as the evenhanded, fair-minded senior political analyst for CNN. I know him as my friend, mentor, and former boss.

I met with David in his office and said, "Senator Obama's campaign has approached me about the job of chief operations officer. I'm torn. I love the work we're doing here at the center and I know there is so much more still to do, but am also intrigued with this possibility. What do you think?"

He didn't hesitate for a moment. "You've got to do it. These opportunities don't come along very often, Betsy. But," he continued, "you have to think very carefully about your friends and colleagues from the Clinton years." He paused, and then said, "You know, something very similar happened to me." And he told me what had occurred to turn *his* life upside down exactly fifteen years earlier.

Although today he identifies himself politically as an independent, David had a long history of affiliation with the Republican Party. He was promoted to head of speech writing for President Nixon at the age of thirty; he advised the Ford administration and was head of communications for President Reagan. Although he played no official role in the George H. W. Bush administration, he was close to the Bush family.

In May of 1993, President Clinton invited David to the White House, and after that visit asked him to join his White House staff as head of communications. (Ironically, he became my sister Dee Dee's boss when she was White House press secretary.) As he has said, it's hard to say no to the president of the United States, and in the middle of 1993, after having worked with a string of Republican administrations, David went to work for the Clinton White House.

"They wanted me to start right away," said David. "It all happened so fast that, as much as I intended to, I just didn't have time to tell any of my former colleagues what was happening. The first time they heard about it was on the news. It really hurt some of those relationships.

"You should do this, Betsy," he said, returning to the question that had brought me to see him. "Don't worry about the center; we'll be fine. Regardless of how far Senator Obama goes, it's too fascinating an opportunity not to do it.

"My only advice, if you do decide to take the job, is to *make sure you let people know.* It's the respectful thing to do, and they'll really appreciate it."

I took Gergen's advice and called many of the people I cared about from my days in the Clinton administration, and wrote personal notes to President and Hillary Clinton. This was not an easy decision, I told them. My time in the Clinton White House had been one of the highlights of my life and I had deep respect and admiration for both the president and Mrs. Clinton. But Senator Obama represented some leadership traits that intrigued me, and the opportunity to participate in this operational capacity was something I couldn't turn down.

Maggie Williams was my first phone call. Maggie had been Hillary Clinton's chief of staff in the White House and later a fellow at the Center for Public Leadership, and I considered her a dear friend as well as a colleague. Eventually (though of course I did not know this back at the time) she would become campaign manager for Hillary's presidential campaign.

A few years later, after the election, I saw Maggie at the swearing-in ceremony of our mutual friend Ann Stock, who had served as White House social secretary during the Clinton administration. Ann was now beginning her new position in the Obama administration as assistant secretary of education and cultural affairs, one of the top posts within the State Department, which was now under the direction of Secretary of State Hillary Clinton. I was so happy to be there to celebrate Ann's new post and to see Maggie and so many other friends and former colleagues. Maggie and I reminisced about that early 2007 phone call. As we hugged each other, she laughed and told my sister Dee Dee, "I gave Betsy permission!"

And it was true: when I contacted Maggie to tell her I was taking a position with the Obama campaign, she let me know that she understood and appreciated what an exceptional opportunity this was. That first phone call gave me the assurance that I wasn't going to lose my relationships with the people I cared about over this new position.

Over the months that followed I stayed in touch with many
of these friends and former colleagues, meeting for dinner or coffee along the campaign trail when possible—and now, eighteen
months later, many of those same relationships would prove to be
important in my efforts to help build unity with the Hillary supporters throughout the summer of 2008.

A CALL FOR UNITY

The first official "unity" event was held on June 26, at Washington, DC's Mayflower Hotel. Barack Obama and Hillary Clinton
were both on hand to address an audience that included nearly 300
of Hillary's fund-raisers and biggest supporters, who had flown in
from all over the country to be there.

Both candidates spoke about the importance of the forthcoming
election and about how they shared the same views for our country.
Senator Clinton was as gracious as Senator Obama was respectful.
As I looked around the room a mixture of feelings was evident:
some people were in tears, some looked visibly uneasy, while others appeared more accepting of the reality of this new alliance. As
difficult as the situation was, it seemed to me that the evening went
as well as possible, and I stayed to the very end, talking with Hillary's supporters, many of them friends and acquaintances of mine.

However, immediately after the event I went across the street
to join a dinner for top Clinton supporters and the senior Obama
finance team at Morton's Steakhouse, hosted by my friend Beth
Dozoretz. (I had known Beth from my Clinton days and she was
a key Hillary supporter who was now strongly committed to the
unity efforts.) The mood and conversation at this dinner were a

sobering reality check. It became clear to me that the depth of frustration and grief went well beyond what our campaign really understood or was prepared to deal with.

For Hillary Clinton's supporters, the end of her candidacy was a deep, intense loss. Some needed a few weeks to grieve while others needed a few months. It was very personal, and no matter what Senator Obama and Senator Clinton herself had said, many were neither ready, willing, nor able to say good-bye so soon.

From that dinner forward, I embarked on a series of unity meetings that became my focus for the rest of that summer.

One of the first such events was a breakfast meeting in late June, at the New York home of Andi Bernstein, who was a member of the Obama National Finance Committee. The meeting was organized by Andi and by Judy Gold, who now served as the Obama campaign's policy chair on women's issues. There were about sixty women in attendance, virtually all of them Hillary supporters, and the featured speaker was Gloria Steinem. I was happy to see her there, as she had been an important mentor to me. Her kind and generous support had helped me to develop credibility with some key women in the women's community during my time in the Clinton White House.

Gloria is not only an icon of women's rights, she also has strong relationships in New York—and she is a compelling speaker. She had been a strong Hillary supporter herself, she reminded the crowd, even though she had publicly praised both candidates. She implored the audience to move on.

"Hillary and Barack agree on virtually every point," she told the group. "And none of us wants to see John McCain elected. I know you are disappointed. But we have to move forward. This election is too important. It's time for us all to pull together."

MILLIONS OF HEARTBROKEN VOTERS

But while Gloria had already processed her disappointment, these women had not. They were not ready to move forward. They were frustrated and angry. Many were heartbroken. It felt personal to them.

There was also a trust issue: many of the Hillary supporters were not comfortable with Senator Obama, his campaign, or how they believed Hillary had been treated or would be treated. This meeting did not go well and only added to the frustration in the room. As Alexis Herman had observed, reflecting on the welfare reform meetings some twelve years earlier:

> When people don't trust you, you really do have to go the extra mile. You have to listen and *gain* their trust before you can even have a conversation.

There were also some specific goals Hillary's supporters wanted to achieve in connection with the Obama campaign. They believed Hillary deserved to be the vice presidential candidate, or at the very least to be considered for the post. They wanted the Obama campaign to help in the efforts to retire her campaign debt. And they wanted the Democratic Convention in August to hold a floor vote with Hillary's name in the ballot.

A floor vote would mean that the convention would go from state to state, asking the delegates, "How many votes for Barack Obama? How many votes for Hillary Clinton?" and so forth. The Hillary supporters wanted her name on the rolls and to have those rolls read out loud. Such a floor vote would be purely symbolic—but the symbolism of it was important. It was the first time in our country's history that a woman had come so close to being selected as the party's presidential candidate. It was an incredibly historic event, and they wanted it to be acknowledged and respected.

But the Obama campaign was reluctant to cede this request. There was some concern that there might be demonstrations at the convention that might embarrass Obama or disrupt the unanimity of the event. In fact, doing anything like that was the furthest thing from these women's minds. Many felt this had been the last chance in their lifetime to see a woman as president of the United States, and at the very least, the moment should be recorded for posterity.

The Obama campaign did finally acquiesce, but not until late in August. Had this gesture of compromise been offered sooner, it likely would have alleviated a significant amount of the discontent. Instead, it continued to fester throughout the summer, all the way to the Democratic Convention in late August.

Ultimately the roll call happened anyway, and Hillary could not have been more gracious. In fact, she was incredibly supportive throughout the summer. She did not push on the vice-presidential nomination. ("I saw Bill go through this, and I know this has to be your decision," she was reported as saying to Senator Obama.) She campaigned across the country endorsing his candidacy strongly and enthusiastically, starting with her concession speech on June 7.

"Every moment wasted looking back keeps us from going forward," Hillary bravely told the Washington, DC, crowd of supporters as she conceded the nomination to Senator Obama. "Life is too short, life is too precious, and the stakes are too high to dwell on what might have been. . . . I will work my heart out to make sure that Barack Obama is our next president."

And she did. One of her close supporters told me at the Democratic Convention that August, "I was still mired in my own sadness and disappointment when I saw Hillary at a recent event, and she was very clear with me: 'I have moved on—and so must you!' "

For many of Hillary's ardent supporters, though, it wasn't that easy. Nearly two months earlier, exit polls in the May 6 Indiana primary showed that fully one-half of Hillary supporters in Indiana would *not* vote for Obama in a general election matchup with John McCain. "A third of Clinton voters said they would pick McCain over Obama," said a CNN report, "while 17 percent said they would not vote at all." Only 48 percent of Clinton supporters said they would back Obama in November.[4]

It was even worse in North Carolina, whose primary fell on the same day. *Fewer than half* of Clinton supporters in that state (only 45 percent) said they would vote for Obama over McCain. Thirty-eight percent said they would vote for McCain, 12 percent said that in the event the contest were between McCain and Obama, they would simply stay home and not vote at all.

These were potentially millions of votes we were talking about. It was clear that we needed to meet the Hillary supporters where they were. And the only way to do that was to start listening.

A WILLINGNESS TO LISTEN

Later that summer I had the opportunity to participate in a unity event in Rhode Island that had a very different feel and outcome.

Hillary Clinton had won the Rhode Island primary handily,

---

4. CNN, May 5, 2008.

and there were a great number of disappointed Hillary supporters
in the state. The small group who planned the event recognized the
need to bring the women of Rhode Island together, and they put
together a guest list of about 120 key Hillary supporters, including Elizabeth Roberts, the state's lieutenant governor (who was
the first woman to hold that post). The event was organized and
hosted by the two cochairs of Rhode Island Women for Obama,
Kelly Taylor, a successful interior designer, and Johnnie Chace, a
prominent Providence developer and philanthropist.

Instead of making financial contribution a condition of attendance, the guests were simply invited to come, no strings at-
tached. As Kelly recalls, "We decided this was not about raising
money; this was about getting everyone together to acknowledge
a shared focus." During that time, Obama supporters in Rhode
Island also made significant outreach to the Hillary supporters
through a series of one-on-one conversations to gain their trust
and understanding, and called people to personally invite them
to the event.

The gathering was held at the Chaces' elegant home as an out-
door reception. It was a beautiful New England summer evening.
Johnnie is a very gracious hostess, and the setting was magical.
The decision to simply bring everyone together, without a fund-
raising agenda, turned out to be the right one. The message of the
evening was, *You matter—and we can't do this without you.*

Johnnie opened the event by welcoming the group, and then
turned the program over to me. I began by sharing with them my
respect and admiration for Hillary Clinton as first lady, US senator, and presidential candidate, along with my sense of the importance of what she had achieved and the difference it would make to
future generations of women, including my own young daughter.

I shared with them something Madison had told me recently as we were walking to her school. "Mommy," she said, "you know what Hillary Clinton taught me? To never give up on your dreams."

"Hillary's dreams of everything she wanted to do as president, of where she wanted to take this country, are the same as Senator Obama's," I added, "and they have now come together to work toward these same goals. Their new partnership on this campaign is very meaningful—and it's also extremely meaningful that you were all willing to be here tonight."

Then Kelly shared some closing remarks. All in all, we spoke for no more than twenty minutes. Mostly what we did was listen and answer questions.

The event had a tangibly positive impact on the group. As Kelly recalls, "From that night forward, our efforts in Rhode Island gained amazing momentum. At the local Obama campaign headquarters, we ran what we called Women Wednesdays, and after that event every one of them was packed."

The Rhode Island chapter of Women for Obama and the Rhode Island women Hillary supporters formed a new partnership together, and Kelly and Johnnie played a key role in this transition. It was their willingness to reach out and listen—the basic human respect they showed these women—that made that evening reception the success that it was.

The Rhode Island event was just one example of what was happening all across the country throughout that summer. The majority of these events were not initiated or organized by campaign headquarters but by individual women taking the initiative to embrace Hillary supporters.

The issue at the heart of the unity effort was a perfect example of something that inevitably confronts every leader. You've probably seen this yourself, in your company or business, and perhaps in your family and friendships as well. In every human organization, differences in points of view inevitably arise, and when they do, it is easy for some to feel their needs are unmet or their voices unheard. It's human nature. And what it takes to address that need and keep the process going is often the simplest gesture of inclusion, listening, and respect.

How to Take the Lead

Respectful leadership means keeping our eyes open to the people around us and making sure they feel truly *heard*. It means approaching everyone we meet from a perspective that says *people matter*. And taking the time to really talk with people and become conscious of what's going on in their lives is more than just a nice way of being: it also gets results.

- Are you willing to listen and let others have their voice, even when it might be inconvenient, difficult, or painful to do so? Listening doesn't mean you have to agree with another's decision or opinion. It simply means being willing to appreciate people for their unique perspective.

- When you find yourself in disagreement with someone, do you focus on making your own views heard, or do you stay open to the other person's views? It's in these situations that truly listening to the other person is especially important—and especially powerful. Genuinely listening, without judgment, keeps the process going.

- In situations of conflict, do you try to win agreement, or do you seek first to establish trust? As Alexis Herman put it, "You can disagree honorably once you have a trust relationship." And nothing establishes trust like genuine listening.

- Do you sometimes feel unheard? If you feel you're being tuned out, examine how you are framing and communicating the issue. What is the best way to frame this issue based on the interests and time demands of the person you're talking to? Given what else that person has on his or her plate, is this the best time for you to bring this issue up? Are you the right person to voice the initiative?

- Do you take care to keep your relationships alive? When you leave a job or move on to other things, take the time and care to keep your connections with former colleagues intact. You never know when you'll be working together again. Taking the time and care to maintain past relationships is a gesture of respect for the other person, and an investment in your own reputation.

4. CLARITY

Torch Relay

In 1984, I spent eight months working for the Olympic Organizing Committee in my hometown of Los Angeles, which happened to be host to the summer Olympics that year. It was my first real job out of college, and it had a lasting impact on me. In fact, there was one day in particular that stands out in memory.

That year, the Olympic torch was flown over the Atlantic from Greece to New York, at which point it was carried on foot by individual runners, creating a relay that stretched across the country to the opening ceremonies in Los Angeles. All told, it was to be an eighty-one-day, 9,000-mile journey. As part of the Olympic torch relay team, four of us working at the Olympic headquarters in Los Angeles were responsible for communicating with the advance team on the ground. It was our job to document exactly which runner would be there every time the torch changed hands, coordinating with the advance team who was managing the course, the crowds, and the media in every town and city along the way.

The torch relay team was just one small part of a massive organization, including the hundreds of people responsible for putting on the event itself in Los Angeles, with people allocated to each individual sport. By that May, staff at the converted airplane hangar that served as Olympic headquarters numbered over one thousand and was growing.

Hosting the Olympic Games is a complex task no matter what year it is, but this year we had an unusual added complication. This was 1984, in the middle of President Ronald Reagan's eight years in office and at the height of the global tensions that dominated the Cold War's final years. On May 8, the day the torch relay was scheduled to begin in New York, an announcement came over the morning news: as a protest against American policies, the Soviet Union was pulling out of the Games.

My friend Judy Biggs, who was assistant director of the torch relay team, remembers hearing the news over the radio on her way in to work that day. "By the time I got to HQ," recalls Judy, "I had gone through a whole gamut of emotions, from shock and horror to deep sadness to all-out rage."

News of the Soviet boycott had affected everyone at headquarters. A sense of uneasy anxiety permeated the day. It was hard to know just what to make of the news: how would this turn of events affect the Olympic Games?

Late that afternoon, a loud siren went off, calling us together. The entire Olympic staff filed into the hangar's vast assembly room, unsure of just what was going on. We watched with anticipation as Peter Ueberroth, the president of the Los Angeles Olympic Organizing Committee, climbed a tall ladder so that everyone could see and hear him. A handsome, striking presence, he radiated a calm confidence.

A highly successful businessman, Ueberroth was something of a legend in the business world, starting when he became vice president of a major airline at the tender age of twenty-two. Earlier in the year, he had been appointed commissioner of baseball by unanimous vote of the twenty-six club owners. (When he actually took office later that year, it was during a Major League Baseball labor conflict, with the umpires union threatening to go on strike. He successfully arbitrated the disagreement in time to finish out the season.) Now here he was, standing at the top of a ladder, facing a thousand discouraged people.

He began by bringing us up to date on the conversations he'd been having since early that morning.

"We've spent the day talking to all the other nations, as well as the sponsors," he told us. All the other countries were still coming to participate in the Games, and none of the sponsors were pulling out. The event was secure—and there were hundreds of athletes from around the world who were still counting on us.

He went on to remind us why we were all here, and what was important about what we were doing together.

"Today's news doesn't change our mission," he said. "We are here to provide the very best opportunity for the great athletes of the world to come together and compete. This is the moment they have spent their entire lives training for and dreaming about. That's why we're here, and that's what we're going to continue doing."

Then he shared the good news about the successful arrival of the Olympic torch in New York. The relay had begun that morning, right on schedule, and the turnout was unbelievable. Huge crowds had gathered to see Gina Hemphill, granddaughter of 1936 Olympian Jesse Owens, and Bill Thorpe Jr., grandson of 1912 Olympian Jim Thorpe, carry the flame, as some 3,600 more runners would do over the next few months on their way across the country.

Twenty minutes after assembling, the group broke up and we all headed back to work. Peter had completely shifted the mood. He instilled in us a renewed sense of pride in our team, reminding each of us why we were here and why it mattered. In the midst of all the rumors, upset, and confusion, what Peter brought to the group was *clarity* and a renewed sense of purpose. People want to feel they are contributing to a cause, to something larger than themselves, and Peter reminded us of that larger cause. I will never forget how he made us feel that day.

That afternoon at HQ was especially memorable, yet it exemplified the way Peter worked every day. Judy recalls another moment, far quieter and less dramatic, that sums up the character of his leadership.

"We were there working really late one night. At one point, I noticed Peter walking out of his office to go talk with someone. I heard a phone ringing off the hook in an empty office nearby. I was on the phone with a torch runner and couldn't pick up, and nobody else was picking up, either. As Peter walked by, he stepped into the office and answered the phone, took down the message for whoever's office it was, and then went on to where he was headed."

Judy remembers this moment, a quarter century later, as if it were yesterday, because of how vividly it represented who Peter was and how he led.

"That simple gesture said we were a *team*, and nobody was too important to answer the phone and take down a message."

Ueberroth strongly believed in "management by walking around," the leadership style Tom Peters had popularized in his landmark book *In Search of Excellence*. I remember him poking his head in the torch relay office often at the end of the day to say "Hi" and acknowledge us for our hard work and long hours.

"Peter always seemed to know when was the exact right moment to stop by and give a compliment or a pat on the back," recalls Judy. "He let us know what a great job we were doing in the moments when things were really tough."

In the days and weeks that followed that May afternoon, we began to realize just how much impact the torch relay was having. It was not merely a success, it lifted the spirits of the whole country.

It had been Peter's idea to run the Olympic torch across the country on foot in a nonstop marathon. Many had greeted this idea with skepticism, but it proved to be a master stroke of innovative leadership. The images of lone runners traversing the miles by day and night with crowds of hundreds turning out everywhere to cheer them on, together with so many stories of personal triumph among the runners, seared themselves into the public's consciousness. The 1984 torch relay created a sense of pride and excitement across the nation. It reminded us—not just those of us at HQ but millions of people across the nation—of our larger sense of national identity.

The Games did go on, and in fact, they turned a profit for the first time in nearly a century. The 1984 Olympics are now regarded as the most financially successful in modern history. By the end of that year, Ueberroth would be hailed as a national hero and named *Time* magazine's "Man of the Year."

Every organization must have a larger purpose, and part of any leader's success is the ability to communicate that purpose with vivid clarity so that it can be passed from person to person within the organization and without—much like a torch being passed from runner to runner across a continent.

WINNING IOWA

Years later, during the 2008 Obama presidential campaign, I saw another example of the importance of bringing clarity to all the

members of an organization. Working closely with campaign manager David Plouffe in the early months of 2007, I watched him
identify and articulate the single core initiative that was necessary
to win this campaign. It would become the campaign's strategic
focus, and it boiled down to two words: *winning Iowa.*

In the US presidential race, Iowa is the first state to hold a caucus or primary, and because of its position on the calendar, the outcome of this one state contest has pivotal impact on the course of
the primary season. We knew that in order to win the party's nomination, we had to come in first or second in the Iowa caucus. Place
third and it would be over. "If Barack doesn't win in Iowa, it is just
a dream," Michelle Obama would say on the campaign trail, and
she was expressing the team's core strategic philosophy.

Assuming we did come in first or second in Iowa, it would also
be important to do well in New Hampshire, the second state on
the primary calendar. All the early states—Iowa, New Hampshire,
South Carolina, and Nevada—were important, and we put significant effort into all of them, especially New Hampshire, which followed Iowa by only five days. But if we lost in Iowa, none of the
rest would matter. Therefore, everything we did had to focus on
that singular point: "How does this help us win in Iowa?"

A major aspect of this focus was the careful balancing of Senator Obama's schedule and prioritizing of his time throughout 2007,
in the months leading up to the primaries. Being relatively new to
the national political scene, he was at somewhat of a disadvantage
in Iowa. Very few people there knew much about him except that
he was a senator from a neighboring state, so it was going to be crit-
ically important to spend significant time there to meet and connect
with the Iowa voters. At the same time, he couldn't spend *all* his
time there. As a sitting senator, he had to participate in the business

of Congress in Washington, and fund-raising goals required that he attend events throughout the country. He couldn't ignore the other early states, either, and it was also important to him that he carve out time to spend with his wife and their two young daughters. A key part of David Plouffe's job was making sure that our strategic focus on Iowa was always reflected in our candidate's schedule. There are ninety-nine counties in Iowa, and over the year leading up to the January caucus, Senator Obama visited every one.

We had past campaigns to learn from, with their lessons both good and bad. From the success of President Bush's 2000 campaign we learned how valuable it can be to bring a business mentality to campaign operations. From Governor Howard Dean's 2004 campaign we learned how powerfully the Internet could be harnessed to raise money.

We also learned what *not* to do in Iowa from the 2004 presidential race. Governor Dean's campaign had generated a lot of excitement, volunteers, and money, but their volunteers were not well organized. As a result, there were a lot of staff and volunteers who had passion and strong intentions, but didn't have the necessary clarity and focus. In fact, the campaign became known for kids in orange hats running around aimlessly—and this did not make a good impression on the Iowa voters.

We were dedicated to doing just the opposite, and under the leadership of Iowa state director Paul Tewes, our volunteers were extremely focused and well organized. We put more resources and paid staff in the state than any presidential campaign had done before, including setting up more than forty offices across the state, nearly three times the number from any previous campaign.

Perhaps as important as what we did were the things we chose *not* to do, always a key factor in any kind of strategic scheduling or budgeting decisions. As one example, early that spring the campaign had an opportunity to be part of a media event in New York City. The Richard LaGravenese film *Freedom Writers*, about a young teacher inspiring a group of at-risk students in an inner-city school, had just been released, and Senator Obama was invited to participate in a special screening to help bring attention to the condition of our educational system. The screening and ensuing Q&A session promised to be a major event, with the participation of the writer/director and possibly a string of A-list celebrities such as Harry Belafonte, Eddie Murphy, and Will Smith.

This would be a worthwhile opportunity for Senator Obama to be part of a forum on an issue he cared about deeply, and there would be quite a few interesting people to meet there, many of whom were his supporters and potentially high-dollar donors. As we began considering the time constraints and logistic issues involved, the decision came down to a simple question: "How does this help us win Iowa?" And the truth was, it didn't—so we didn't go forward with it.

We all face situations like this in our organizations and our individual lives, where we have to weigh many competing demands and opportunities. It can seem difficult, if not overwhelming, unless we have that kind of clarity about our larger objectives. One way to help create and hold that clarity is to have our own version of that focusing question: "How does this help us win Iowa?"

This organizational focus and discipline paid off for the campaign. Starting as a relatively unknown candidate, Senator Obama achieved a nine-point win in Iowa, going from a long shot to a serious presidential contender, all in less than a year.

TRANSFORMING AN AGENCY

Over the course of my years in the Clinton administration, I experienced what a difference this kind of strategic clarity can make. My first job in Washington was with the Small Business Administration (SBA), where I served for nearly two years as director of the Office of Women's Business Ownership before going to work at the newly created White House Women's Office. Then, after two years at the White House, I was recruited back to the SBA to take a senior management post there.

This sequence had the effect of creating an interesting kind of symmetry, with work at the SBA at both the beginning and end of my time in the Clinton administration. Both times we had an ambitious agenda for the economic empowerment of the nation's small businesses and entrepreneurs. Both times the president had appointed a dedicated, talented leader committed to carry out that agenda. Yet despite this apparent symmetry, the results were dramatically different, and the reason for that contrast boils down to a critical difference in clarity.

When I first arrived at the SBA in September 1993, the agency was a place that, historically, had not been well regarded. By the time I left in June 1995 for the White House, the agency had been transformed. In less than two years it had become a genuinely exciting place to work, a place that people all over Washington were talking about. The main reason for that transformation was the man President Clinton brought in to run the agency, Erskine Bowles.

"People said being in the SBA was like being stationed in Guam," says Erskine, speaking of how things were when he first arrived. "Nobody wanted to say they worked at the SBA; they preferred just to say they worked 'for the federal government.'"

President Clinton wanted to change that. He thought small business mattered, and he wanted the agency to play a more integral role in the administration's economic goals. Toward that end, he invited in a successful businessman from the private sector to take the agency's reins.

This was far from the traditional definition of SBA administrator, as that agency's top post is called. The last several people to fill this position had been career politicians. Erskine, on the other hand, was an accomplished entrepreneur with an ability to get things done. Fresh out of college, he went to work for Morgan Stanley and before long launched his own highly successful investment firm. He was exactly the kind of person the president wanted to run the SBA. Erskine in turn worked to fill the agency's management positions with experienced business owners.

As director of the Office of Women's Business Ownership, my new job was to be the administration's liaison and advocate for women business owners. This was a perfect fit for me because I had been a business owner myself, in the insurance and financial services sector, and the majority of my clients had been women business owners.

During my years in business, I had seen how directly the success or failure of a small business is tied to the availability of credit. Small businesses often have difficulty gaining access to capital, and this is far tougher for women and minorities, who were (and still are today) the fastest-growing segment of the small-business community. Hillary Clinton used to describe stories she'd heard from women entrepreneurs who were unable to get the credit they needed to start or grow their businesses. "How many women's business dreams," Hillary would say, "are dashed in bank parking lots?"

I had experienced this difficulty myself during my years in business, and had turned to the same solution as so many women business owners do: funding my business using credit cards. Some of my clients had put as much as $100,000 on credit cards to finance their businesses.

From my first day on the job, Erskine was quite clear on what my mission was: find a way to give women entrepreneurs more access to capital.

At the time, the SBA was providing an 80 to 90 percent guarantee for small-business loans that banks considered too risky to fund purely on their own. (As the single largest financial backer of American business, the SBA often serves as the "lender of last resort.") However, for a variety of reasons this process was not working effectively for women business owners, who were securing only 8 percent of those loans.

We came up with an idea for turning the process around, based on a concept that had been tried at the agency years before (in that earlier case, for disaster relief). Instead of getting the SBA involved only after the business owner was sitting at the bank applying for the loan, why not work with the individual business owners earlier on, making sure they were adequately prepared with a solid business plan and good credit rating, and prequalify them? That way, by the time they were walking into the bank office, they would *already* have our backing.

That is exactly what we did. We started the Women's Prequalification Loan Program as a pilot program in sixteen cities, and eventually put it in place throughout the nation. During President Clinton's second term the program was also expanded to include veterans, minorities, and the disabled community.

The program was very successful. What made it especially gratifying were the personal stories we heard from women across the country. With our support, they told us, they were able to obtain bank loans, and this made a substantial difference in their business success and their confidence. Owing in part to this program, the overall loan volume for women business owners that year increased from 8 percent to 20 percent, for a total of 7,211 loans totaling $1.7 billion.

ONE PRIORITY . . . AMONG FORTY

In early 1997, with the 1996 reelection behind us and President Clinton's second term under way, the president's agenda shifted from reelection to legacy, and my role shifted as well. Leaving the White House Women's Office, I returned to the SBA to take a new position there, and a big part of the reason for this decision was the agency's new administrator, Aida Alvarez.

Aida is an outgoing woman with a vivacious personality. Born in Puerto Rico to very modest means, she later moved with her family to New York, earned her bachelor of arts from Harvard (graduating *cum laude*) and became a news anchor and award-winning journalist, earning an Emmy nomination for her reporting on guerilla activities in El Salvador before going on to an equally colorful career in investment banking, public service, and administration. When President Clinton appointed her to run the SBA at the beginning of 1997, she became the first Puerto Rican and the first Hispanic woman to hold a cabinet-level post.[1]

As administrator, one of the first things Aida did was to meet

---

1. Under Clinton, this was also the first time an SBA administrator was elevated to a cabinet-level position; the position was demoted again during the Bush administration.

with former SBA staff people. I remember having lunch together in the White House mess and discussing her new post. Her energy and enthusiasm were infectious. Later on, after our conversation, she called me with the idea of my returning to the SBA as part of her senior team, where I could play a role in the next chapter of welfare reform. This was one of the president's six "legacy goals," and Aida believed that small business could play a significant role.

Hard as it may be these days to imagine or remember, the economy was doing so well at the time that unemployment was very low and small businesses were actually having difficulty finding workers. The president's lasting impact on welfare reform would depend on the availability of jobs and how readily people transitioning off welfare could find them. Given this situation, thought Aida, why not partner state welfare offices with SBA offices and work together to help these people secure jobs? It seemed a natural fit. With our support, more women might also be able to start their own businesses.

I agreed to take the position, in part because it offered a way to help implement the president's Welfare to Work effort. Having worked at the agency before, I had relationships with many of the SBA state directors who would be responsible for implementing our new initiative. It was an innovative idea, and many of them were open and willing to participate with us.

We got off to a very good start, with lots of enthusiasm and support from the state directors . . . but over the next few years progress became more difficult. Welfare to Work was gradually joined by additional initiatives that the administrator championed, and as the list grew, the state directors and agency staff began losing clarity about where to put their focus. "What are the budget priorities? Which are our most important initiatives? Where should I put my time?" These were questions to which we did not have clear answers. Welfare to Work went from being a priority to being just one of dozens of initiatives—and this took its toll.

What struck me about this situation was the difference it made in agency morale. I saw people become frustrated as their time and energy became diluted. It was hard to make substantial progress in any one area, and as a result, people didn't feel a sense of accomplishment about their individual contributions. Spirits began to sag.

None of this reflected any lack of skills on Aida's part. On the contrary, she had extraordinary talents and personal strengths: she was committed, persuasive, energetic, and charismatic. Her passion for serving the agency and the president led to a robust agenda. In fact, she did what so many leaders unintentionally do in their earnest desire to have a significant impact: they dilute the mission with competing demands.

The missing ingredient was *clarity of focus*—which was exactly the key ingredient Erskine had brought to the agency.

THREE WORDS: "ACCESS TO CAPITAL"

Under Erskine, everybody at the SBA knew exactly what they were doing when they came to work each morning. Just as David Plouffe would spell out our agenda at the Obama campaign fourteen years later in two words, *winning Iowa,* Erskine made it crystal clear that our mission at the SBA boiled down to three: *access to capital.* Whatever your specific job or title at the agency, your top priority was making sure that your actions served the goal of *access to capital* for America's small business owners. Of course, the agency had other obligations and initiatives—but there was never any confusion about what was our top priority.

"It was all about being focused and precise," recalls Amy Millman, who was director of the National Women's Business Council (which is housed at the SBA) during Erskine's tenure. "He was very clear about his expectations. It made us all better teammates and we were more productive."

Erskine's expectations for his weekly staff meetings came down to twelve words, which I still remember today, all these years later: "Don't give me anything more than two pages—and be on time." Being even five minutes late was not an option.

Here is how Erskine recounts a conversation he had with the president when he went to work for him as chief of staff during the president's second term:

"When I went to the White House, I told the president, 'I'm not a vision guy. I've never had a vision in my life. You have a hundred of them a day! But you can't accomplish all that. You've got to sit down and pick out three or four things—and if you do, I can help you make them real.'

"We adopted the idea that less is more: instead of trying to do a bunch of different things every day, we decided to do one thing a week—but then we would really *do* it."

The clarity of purpose Erskine brought to the SBA created such success that total loans to small business increased by 80 percent during his tenure. The positive feedback from the business community, along with acknowledgment from Congress and the White House, instilled a pride in the agency that had not been there in years.

LIVING WITH AN OUTBOX STRATEGY

David Gergen was speaking once at the Center for Public Leadership about the strengths and weaknesses of George H. W. Bush's presidency, and he said something I'll never forget: "The Bush

White House approached things with more of an inbox strategy than an outbox strategy." They had been so consumed and distracted by all the issues coming at them that they were never able to formulate or implement their own vision.

I've seen this time and time again: part of what makes a leader effective at her job is the ability to help people become clear about which tasks are essential to the goal—and which are not. As Jim Collins puts it, "*Stop doing* lists are more important than *to do* lists."

No one can do it all—but we all know people who try. We have all seen family, friends, or colleagues who consistently stay late at the office or work weekends to "catch up" on their work. Sometimes it's unavoidable, given project deadlines or unusual circumstances, but it has always seemed to me that people who consistently stay at the office until 10:00 or 11:00 at night either don't delegate or have difficulty prioritizing. Either way, it's not something to wear as a badge of honor.

I remember admiring George Stephanopoulos, then White House senior adviser, for his ability to leave the White House most nights at a reasonable hour. George was there early every morning and put in a full day, even by White House standards, but he was committed to going to the gym every day after work. Everyone was pretty clear that if you needed George, you'd better reach him before 6:30 or 7:00 p.m. No one thought less of him for it; in fact, there was much respect for him, and his position and portfolio only grew during his six years there. He knew how to set boundaries for his life, to prioritize and get his work done.

Living with an *inbox strategy,* as David Gergen put it, means we respond to every phone call or email, request or interruption as they come at us. It means we put ourselves at the mercy of others' needs and agendas. It's so easy to get lost in the details and responsibilities of our lives. For example, one common complaint I hear is how easily people lose precious hours of their day swallowed up in their email. Living with an inbox strategy, we often find ourselves at the end of the day wondering where the time went and why we didn't seem to accomplish anything.

Living with an *outbox strategy* means taking control of our day by setting clear and focused goals and then following that road map to get the work done.

My sisters and I first learned this from our father. During most of my childhood my dad was an executive at Lockheed, where we watched him go from test pilot to vice president of quality. He is a very focused person: every day before he left work, he would make a list of the top ten items he planned to accomplish the next day, in order of priority. When he arrived at work each morning, he would hit the ground running, with a focused clarity about what needed to happen that day, and in what order.

My dad also taught us how important it is to be on time—such a simple thing, yet such a critical part of bringing clarity and focus to your day. "If you're on time, you're fifteen minutes late!" he would say. Trained as a navy pilot, he'd had to arrive early before every flight to prepare, and, as he often told us, "This translates to everything else."

Effective leaders arrive early so that they can be prepared for the meeting or event, find their place in the room and calmly go over their notes or prepared remarks for the meeting. Running in late, out of breath and with papers flying everywhere, doesn't impress your colleagues with your busy schedule. It just creates the impression that you are disorganized and possibly incompetent.

Although I have often struggled with being late, squeezing in that last phone call or glancing one more time at my email, my dad's advice has always rung in my ears. After all these years, I have to admit he is right. When I am early, things run much smoother, there is little or no stress, and I am therefore much calmer—and so are the people around me.

Another person who taught me the importance of focus and clarity was John Davies, who ran the Massachusetts Mutual Life Insurance Company office in Los Angeles where I spent several years early in my career selling insurance and financial products.

What I remember most about John was his uncluttered office and immaculately clean desk. He started each day with nothing on his desk but a blank sheet of lined paper, on which he would write his outline for the day. Several lines were for agency work; several were for the prospecting calls he would make for new agents or for his personal sales; several more were for appointments; and a few were for the people in his life he cared about, whom he planned to connect with that day.

In the course of his day, John would fill in that sheet with the calls and appointments he completed. It is no surprise that, before becoming the area's general agent at only thirty-seven, he had been one of MassMutual's top-producing agents himself.

"If you see three people every day," he would tell us, "then you'll sell three policies a week. And if you make ten calls a day, you'll set up three new appointments. If you make ten phone calls and see three people a day, there's no way you cannot succeed in this business.

"You don't finish the day till you've made your ten calls and seen your three appointments," he would add. "If you're here at eight in the morning, and you make your calls, set your appointments, and see your three people, and it's still only noon, you can go to the beach!"

However, what most people did was wander in around 9:30, have coffee, chat with colleagues, then eventually get into their office and spend the next few hours on paperwork, then go to lunch . . . and before they knew it, it'd be 2:00—and they hadn't seen one prospect or created a single new appointment. (I was guilty of this myself sometimes.) A few months of days like that, and anyone would be completely discouraged.

Whenever an agent would start talking about leaving the agency over lack of sales, John would ask, "How many appointments did you have this week?" and the answer would invariably be two or one—or none. No wonder they hadn't made any sales!

It didn't take me long to realize that when I was focused and followed John's plan, my business grew—and when I didn't, it didn't.

That's the beauty and power of clarity: it allows you to know exactly what you need to do to succeed. Then, all you have to do is *do* it.

KEEP COMMUNICATION LINES OPEN

How well we are able to create and maintain clarity of task and purpose with our teams depends, of course, on how well we communicate with them. The clearest vision and strategy in the world doesn't accomplish much if we're not able to convey it to others in a way that they understand. It is also important to keep the communication going consistently, so that your team remains inspired and engaged. I learned this firsthand when I was executive director of the Center for Public Leadership.

One day, I traveled together with Donna Kalikow, my deputy, to a leadership event in New York. As we chatted throughout our trip about various aspects of the center, to my amazement, she shared with me the fact that she was not really clear on the strategic mission of the center.

This was an eye-opener for me. David Gergen and I had just held a strategic staff retreat several months earlier, and we believed everyone was fully on board with our focus on personal and interpersonal leadership development. Yet here was my deputy, who had participated in these activities and held a leadership position at the center—and *she* was still unclear about our mission!

As leaders and managers, we can never take for granted that everyone is clear and on the same page. We can't assume that because we have mentioned it once, people are on board or will stay on board.

My friend Georgette Mosbacher, the savvy CEO of Borghese, a high-end cosmetics company, makes it a priority to communicate with all her employees, and not just the top management. "If people understand what you expect from them," says Georgette, "you won't often be disappointed. It's when they don't know, when you aren't clear or haven't communicated your expectations, that problems happen."

Every Thursday, Georgette holds meetings with all her department heads. Because she personally designed the format and structure of the weekly reports, the information they give her is exactly what she needs to run the company. Every department head is completely clear on the data the reports track, what is expected of them, and what success looks like, for them and for their department.

But communicating with department heads is not enough, says Georgette. She wants to make sure every employee in the company knows exactly what is going on.

"When we have a new product," says Georgette, "I bring everyone in and give them each a full-size sample. Even if they're only involved in filling the bottles, I want them to know what's in the bottle, what the artwork looks like, what the ad's going to look like, everything about it. They understand what the finished product is—and it makes them feel more a part of the process and part of the team."

Keeping everyone fully informed, Georgette points out, also makes a stronger company that is far better prepared to handle problems when they come up. When people don't know what is going on, says Georgette, they start to wonder, and that's when tension mounts and rumors spread.

"If there's a problem, I bring everyone in and explain it. Informed people feel secure. People will pull together, even in a crisis, if they all understand what's going on and what's at stake. It's the not knowing, the darkness, that scares us.

"This is as true in a family as it is in a business. If something's happening—Dad loses his job, or Mom is sick—it's better to sit down and explain it, because no matter what the problem is, people's imagination is always going to be worse than it really is."

When Jack Welch, former CEO of GE, came to speak to students at the Kennedy School, he confided to us that every quarter he would give feedback to each of his department heads in the form of handwritten letters. He did this, he said, to make sure there was absolute clarity, direct from the boss, about what was on track and what needed to be improved. Like Georgette Mosbacher's team, Jack Welch's department heads were crystal clear on what success in their departments looked like.

In many organizations, there is often no clear feedback on people's performance until something goes wrong—and by then it's usually too late to deal with the issue effectively.

Georgette and Jack are very different people, with different leadership styles and different companies, but they both put clear mechanisms in place to ensure that they would identify problems early on. Exactly what feedback mechanism we have is less important than the fact that we *have* one. If we don't, even small mistakes can snowball to a crisis point, as I learned early in my career, when I joined Irene Tritschler's fund-raising team.

CLEARLY COMMUNICATE EXPECTATIONS

In 1985, a year after being part of the Olympic torch relay team, I went to work for the reelection campaign of Tom Bradley, the charismatic African-American mayor of Los Angeles. Bradley made a huge impression on me. There was something both elegant and personable about him, something deeply authentic, that made us all feel incredibly devoted to him. Ali Webb, his press secretary, says it beautifully: "His leadership goal was to be *mayor of all the people,* and as corny as that may sound, that was the aspiration he set for himself and for all of us on his staff."

It was while working as part of Mayor Bradley's campaign advance team that I met Irene Tritschler, who had worked for many years as his exclusive fund-raiser. After Bradley's successful reelection bid, Irene decided to expand her business and take on more clients. When she recruited me to join her new fund-raising team, I was assigned to work on an annual fund-raiser for then state senator Art Torres.

As the date drew near, I began to panic. There were many details yet undone, and it became clear both to me and to others that I was in over my head. By three days before the event, the situation had become urgent, and Irene and other members of the team had to halt their other activities in order to focus their full attention on the Torres event. In the end, to my relief, the event was successful, and Senator Torres and his team were happy with the results. However, it had not gone smoothly from our end, and soon after the event, I was fired.

It was, to say the least, an early life lesson for me in clarity. I had not understood the extent of my job responsibilities, and being new to political fund-raising, I didn't even know what I didn't know. There was no clear check-in or feedback mechanism in place, so the extent of the problem didn't become clear until it was an emergency and almost too late to fix.

Ken Blanchard often says, "The key to developing people is to catch them doing something right." But some leaders too often focus on catching people doing things *wrong*. When you give constant feedback and are dedicated to catching people doing things right, you can identify and correct errors early on. Your people will also feel more valued and supported.

Irene and I remained friends and reflected back on this episode a few years later. The key learning for both of us was twofold: Irene had not been clear enough about my exact job duties and the time line for those duties. For my part, I hadn't asked for help.

As Georgette pointed out, clarity is just as important in personal relationships as it is in business. It is easy to make assumptions about other people's expectations, about what matters to them or what makes them feel appreciated—but again, assumptions can often be wrong. The only reliable way to gain that clarity is to ask.

A marriage therapist once told me that one strategy for a happy marriage is to ask your partner or spouse what makes them feel loved. We often love someone the way *we* like to be loved, she said, or show our appreciation by doing those things that *we* would want done. As an example, she told this story:

> A woman once organized a surprise party for her husband's fiftieth birthday. He was expecting a quiet evening together over a romantic dinner at their favorite restaurant. But when they walked in the place—*Surprise!*—there were all their friends waiting for them.
>
> He was surprised, all right. The next day he told her that he appreciated the gesture and had a good time at the party—but that he would have preferred a quiet evening with just the two of them.
>
> She was so disappointed! She had spent months planning the evening and it had taken a tremendous effort to pull off. If the roles were reversed and he had thrown her a surprise party like this, she knew she would have felt completely loved and appreciated.

Asking the people in our lives, both personal and professional, what is important to them and what makes them feel loved or valued, can give us precious insight into how best to nurture those relationships, and prevent many potential misunderstandings and disappointments. It can make the difference between a successful relationship and a failed one.

I recently asked my daughter, Madison, what made her feel most loved. Her answer was, "When we spend time together, just me and you—and no cell phones."

LEADING WITH QUESTIONS

It's one thing for the leader to be clear on goals, objectives, and time lines, but that doesn't necessarily translate to the team by sheer force or top-down mandate. Achieving clarity and focus throughout an organization requires a dedication to getting both input and buy-in from the rest of the team by leading with questions.

When he assumed his post at the SBA, Erskine Bowles could see that the organization needed to make some significant shifts in how it operated. However, rather than simply step in and make sweeping changes in a unilateral way, he wanted first to take the pulse of all the people who would be affected. "To get something done in any organization," as he told me recently, "you have to have buy-in from the troops." In this case, this meant hearing not only from his own staff at the SBA but also from the small-business community throughout the nation.

He attended a series of town halls in every region of the country, including state and regional SBA managers and state directors together with local small business owners. Hundreds of people came to each town hall. Rather than just stand up and talk, he spent the majority of each meeting listening. Not only did he want to get other people's buy-in, he also wanted to get their input and learn more about exactly what changes were needed to set the direction of the agency.

One of the key complaints Erskine heard during these meetings was that the paperwork associated with an SBA loan was too complicated. Accordingly, under his leadership the SBA developed a streamlined one-page application for loans under $100,000 (called "Low Doc") and cut the form for amounts over $100,000 from more than forty pages down to six. This also made the whole process of securing an SBA loan less intimidating to the applicant, which also meant lower processing costs and faster turnaround for the bank.

"Modifying our products and streamlining the lending paperwork," says Erskine, "was not something I thought up. It happened because we listened to our customers and our employees."

After his years in the Clinton administration Erskine was named president of the University of North Carolina, an educational system that included seventeen different campuses, and the situation he found there was similar in some ways to that of the SBA. "They all knew we had to change," says Erskine, "but none of them really *wanted* to change. I had a sense of what needed to be done, but I also knew I didn't have the credibility with this group to get it done. I'm not an academic, I'm just a business guy."

So he employed the same tactic as he had at the SBA, holding some thirty town hall meetings throughout North Carolina. He asked the most respected professors from each campus to serve on a special panel in each meeting along with a group of prominent businesspeople from the area. Everyone who participated came away with a shared clarity about what needed to happen, which effectively paved the way for Erskine to begin putting those changes into effect. The results were so impressive that university administrators from around the country started visiting so they could see for themselves what North Carolina was doing. It was accomplishments such as this that later prompted President Obama to appoint Erskine as cochair of his bipartisan panel on deficit reduction.

Leadership is not about having all the answers; it is about asking the questions. The clarity Erskine achieves comes from listening to the people in the field—which is ultimately an expression of his respect for them. He doesn't go into an organization with all the answers ready at hand. Quite the opposite: it is only by asking the questions that he has been able to see what needs to be done—and gained the necessary support to *get* it done.

BEING CLEAR ON YOUR *WHY*

I want to close this chapter with one more Erskine Bowles story that is not about strategic clarity but about the underlying value that clarity serves.

When I traveled from Los Angeles to Washington in the summer of 1993 to interview for a possible position in the Clinton administration, I met Erskine for the first time. He already had a stellar reputation, and I was very excited to be meeting with him. As we sat together, he asked me, "After six years in business, you must be just starting to do quite well and have a good client base. What would make you consider leaving now to come work for the SBA?"

He was right, but I believed that this was a unique opportunity to advocate for *all* women business owners instead of just my own client base. (I also planned to return to my business after two years at the SBA, although, of course, that never happened.)

I was curious about him, too, so I asked, "What about you? What made you leave behind *your* successful business in North Carolina to come work here?"

By way of answering, he told me this story.

In the months leading up to the election, a friend of Erskine's had enrolled him in helping then governor Clinton's campaign by putting on a fund-raiser. Scheduled to ride with Clinton to the event, Erskine was uncharacteristically late getting to their meeting point.

At the time, in addition to his full-time professional life, Erskine was also serving as international president of the Juvenile Diabetes Research Foundation and was active in his efforts to help forward the cause of stem cell research to find a cure. This was a cause he was personally devoted to: his own son Sam suffered from the disease. As it happened, Sam had experienced a low-blood-sugar seizure that day—and that was what had made Erskine late for his appointment with the governor.

"If you've ever seen something like that, then you know," says Erskine, recalling the day. "It just rips your heart out. We got Sam stabilized so he was okay, but I didn't get to the governor's car until really late.

"It was just the two of us in the backseat, and Clinton asked me, 'Erskine, you seem kind of blue today. What's wrong?'

"I told him about Sam. 'And what makes me doubly mad,' I said, 'is President Bush vetoing the fetal tissue research bill, after it passed the Senate 87 to 10 with even Jake Garn and Strom Thurmond voting for it. All the experts are telling me this is the best hope for a cure for children like Sam, and that they've got it totally separated from the abortion issue. There's no good reason to stonewall it—but that's what's happening, and it's all politics.'

"Well, he didn't say a word. I remember thinking, Gosh, this guy is supposed to be so empathetic! But I let it go. I figured he had a lot on his mind.

"About three weeks later, he made his major health-care speech at Merck, and in that speech he said: 'I have a friend, a businessman from North Carolina, and he has a son he loves more than life itself, and who has juvenile diabetes. He's convinced me that we need to take the politics out of scientific research. If I'm elected president, I'm going to lift the ban on fetal tissue research.'

"He never told me he was going to do this, never said a thing to me about it. The only reason I even knew about it was that someone from the foundation read about it and told me.

"After the election the president invited me to a reception at the White House. At the reception, he asked me to join him in the Oval Office, and when I got there he took out a pen, handed it to me, and said, 'Erskine, I used this pen yesterday to sign a proclamation lifting the ban on fetal tissue research. I want you to take it home and give it to Sam, and tell him there's hope for a cure.'

"I called him back that night, and told him I wanted to work for him, and that I'd go wherever he put me."

By the time Erskine had finished his story, there were tears in his eyes, and in mine, too.

As important as it is for us to be clear on the *how* of a task or goal, there is something even more important: to be clear on the *why*.

How to Take the Lead

One of a leader's most crucial roles is to hold clarity for the team. This means being clear on your organization's larger purpose, and looking for ways to communicate that purpose with such vivid clarity that it will transmit from person to person both within the organization and without, like a torch being passed from runner to runner across a continent.

- Every task, goal, or effort, whether of an individual or an organization, needs a clear focal point. What is your organization's version of the focusing question, *How does this help us win Iowa?*

- Too many competing goals and initiatives can kill momentum and morale. Of all your priorities, what is your number one top priority? Is your team or organization clear about where to focus their daily time and energy? What is your version of Erksine Bowles's *access to capital*?

- Do you work with an inbox strategy or an outbox strategy? In other words, do you spend the bulk of your time reacting to whatever comes at you, or do you start each day by setting clear and focused goals for what *you* want to accomplish and then follow that road map throughout the day?

- Do you have clearly established boundaries for when you are *on,* and when you are off? Does your work run you, or do you run your work?

- Do you arrive at events early, or run in late because you were trying to squeeze in that extra phone call, email, or errand?

- Do you communicate the big picture clearly and often? The clearest vision and strategy in the world doesn't accomplish much if you don't convey it to others in a way that they understand. It's also important to keep the communication going consistently, so that your team *remains* inspired and engaged.

- Are you clearly communicating your expectations to the people around you? As Georgette Mosbacher says, "It's when you aren't clear or haven't communicated your expectations that problems happen." Does your team know what success looks like?

- Are you communicating with *everyone* in the organization (group, business, family)? When people are kept fully informed, then they will pull together, even in a crisis.

- Do you have a feedback mechanism in place, so that you learn about problems early on, when they're relatively easy to fix, rather than letting them snowball to a crisis point? Do you have a strategy for catching your people doing something right?

- Do you consistently look for answers in the field? Asking your people for input not only creates buy-in from the field, it also connects you to some of the best information and insight you can get. Leadership is not about having all the answers—it is about being willing to ask the questions.

5. COLLABORATION

The Joy of Jamming Together

O ne of the simple truths of leadership is that we rarely get anything significant done on our own. The old command-and-control style of leadership was a model that said, "I know what needs to be done, now do what I say." The new model of leadership appreciates the fact that no man or woman is an island, and that genuine accomplishment is the result of teamwork, not the lone feat of a single unaided hero.

"The overplaying of individual leadership is a tricky thing," says Marshall Ganz, "because most effective leaders work in collaboration with others. This myth that floats around of the talented solo genius is simply not true."

The myth of the lone leader isn't just inaccurate, it can actually be hurtful. So often people hesitate to step up and take a leadership role simply because they are uncomfortable with the idea of having to be the one with all the answers. But that's not what effective leadership is about today. Effective leadership is about collaboration, and collaboration is about inclusion. In an atmosphere of genuine collaboration, people feel they are an integral part of the larger process.

Genuine collaboration doesn't mean *looking like* you're being open to different points of view—it means actually *being* open to those points of view, and even seeking them out. Some of our best solutions and life lessons come from those with significantly different perspectives from our own.

UNSEEN THREADS OF CONTINUITY

One day in the late spring of 2001, I arrived at my office at the Kennedy School and found a voice-mail message from a woman who introduced herself as Lezlee Westine.

"I'm the new head of Public Liaison for the Bush White House," she explained, "and I need your help!"

Lezlee had just moved east from California to start her new position (much as I had done exactly eight years earlier), and now found herself in the midst of an uproar from women leaders in Washington. Most of these women were Democrats, and they were upset by the sudden closing of the White House Women's Office.

"I've been bombarded by calls from the women's constituency," Lezlee continued. "I was hoping you could give me a call and fill me in on a little history here?"

I returned Lezlee's call and we spoke for a few minutes. I shared with her my background at the Women's Office. When she asked if I might be willing to meet with her in person, I said, "Of course!"

A few weeks later I made the trip from Boston to Washington to meet with Lezlee. It was uncanny how much we shared in common: two California girls, exactly the same age—in fact, our birthdays were just one week apart. We hit it off immediately.

Over a long lunch at the Oval Room, a favorite eating place located just a few blocks from the White House, Lezlee and I discussed the differences in how the George W. Bush White House approached her office and how those differences might impact her job.

For one thing, the new administration had significantly reduced the number of staff assigned to Public Liaison. Most people don't realize that the White House has a set number of staff each president can work with. They can be rearranged, but you can't simply add new staff without that addition being part of a congressionally approved budget. Karl Rove, President Bush's senior adviser, had now reorganized this part of the White House staff to create his Office of Strategic Initiatives. In addition to closing the Women's Office altogether, this shift in priorities had drastically reduced Lezlee's staff, leaving her with eight people—a third of the two dozen Alexis Herman had in the Clinton days to accomplish the same job.

A committed advocate of women's issues, Lezlee was shocked when she first learned that the Women's Office was being closed. "I was at a basketball game," she said, "and Ari Fleischer [the president's press secretary] calls me up and says, 'Lezlee, we closed the Women's Office; you're now head of women's outreach.' I said, only half jokingly, 'What?! Why didn't you tell me this *before* we closed the office?!'"

I walked her through the mission and accomplishments of the Women's Office, the network of women leaders in Washington, and the relationships we forged with cabinet secretaries and political appointees. As our lunch wound to a close, Lezlee surprised me with this question:

"Betsy, would you be willing to come to the White House and cohost a meeting with me? Say, in the next few weeks? It would be an opportunity for you to introduce me to the women's constituency groups and help me begin the conversation about how we might work together." She continued excitedly, "What do you think?"

In the transition from a Democratic to a Republican administration, or vice versa, there is a significant shift of personnel and
culture. This was an example where one individual took the initiative to create a relationship that provided a thread of continuity.

EXPLORING AREAS OF AGREEMENT

The following month, we held the meeting Lezlee had proposed.
I remember her grace and warmth as she opened the discussion,
saying that although we would not all agree on every issue, there
was more we did agree on than there was that we didn't. Her main
objective that day was to communicate her willingness to collaborate with the women's community and to build mutual trust. Her
clarity and honesty about what she could and could not promise
was a breath of fresh air.

"I don't want to waste the next four years in contentious dialogue," she told the group. "Let's not spend our time concen-
trating on areas of disagreement. For example, I happen to be
pro-choice—but the president is not, so we're not going to have
agreement on that issue. The question is, what are the areas where
we *can* move forward? I think we could certainly make progress on
economic security, health, and education issues."

We went around the room and the women leaders shared their
top priorities. There was a positive and open dialogue throughout
the meeting. When she talks now about the initiatives that eventually bore fruit during her tenure, Lezlee credits that initial meeting
with the women leaders.

"It was our lunch together that gave me not only an idea of
what to do but also the courage to do it," Lezlee told me recently.

"The approach we set out during that lunch together was so constructive—and so *not* partisan."

It was Lezlee's willingness to explore the history of her office and to seek out help from across the aisle that made that meeting possible. It was easy to be nonpartisan and freely share my experience and knowledge with her; Lezlee *made* it easy. It was a privilege to spend that time with her. We went on to establish a friendship that remains to this day.

What's more, she got *results*.

"A lot of events came out of that initial meeting," she told me recently. "I developed a plan and created an interagency working group. This was one of several ways that we reached out and collaborated with other women in the administration.

"We held a women's entrepreneurship summit, we did many briefings for the women's constituencies, and we were able to get Mrs. Bush and Condi Rice to *Fortune* magazine's Most Powerful Women conference. We did a lot that wasn't so visible to the public eye but that had very positive consequences."

Lezlee's work in her White House role was an inspiring example of collaborative leadership. Because she took the time to build those relationships across the aisle, she was able to accomplish a good deal more than she might have otherwise.

THREE STEPS TO EFFECTIVE COLLABORATION

Collaboration is an essential part of leadership, but the process doesn't stop there. Effective leadership also means being willing to be the one who takes clear action. After gathering and listening to all the different perspectives and input, a leader is responsible for

taking decisive action based on the insights gleaned from that collaboration.

There is still one more step in the process. After listening and
making a clear decision, an effective leader then *clearly communi-
cates* that decision out to the troops, including what the decision
is, why it was made, and what it means to the organization and
to each individual involved. Again, a big part of implementing a
strong strategy is getting buy-in from the team—and the only way
you'll secure people's buy-in is if you clearly and fully communicate with them.

A friend of mine holds a senior management position with a
major technology business based on the East Coast. In 2009, the
company went through a few rounds of layoffs and the remaining
employees were asked to do much more with much less. No ex-
planation was given, no words of encouragement or appreciation.
The company then announced they were cutting everyone's salary
by 5 percent and discontinuing company contributions to the retirement plans. This news was communicated in an email.

My friend was incensed. "We keep getting blindsided," she told
me. "They don't respect us enough to tell us in person, explain
what's happening or why, or give us any idea of how long they expect this situation to last."

They were left in the dark. As a result, she now has no enthusiasm for her work. "I do the bare minimum and no more," she confessed. "I've lost all my energy for my job."

This sort of situation is so common—and so unnecessary. I
heard a vivid example of how differently this situation could have
been managed when I sat in on Stephanie Hickman Boyse's talk at
a spring 2010 leadership conference at the University of Michigan,
where we were both speakers.

GAINING BUY-IN THROUGH BAD TIMES

Stephanie is president and CEO of Brazeway, Inc., a large manufacturer of air-conditioning and refrigeration components. Started by Stephanie's grandfather in 1946, Brazeway is the world's largest producer of frost-free evaporator coils. (Unless you happen to own a Samsung fridge, you have a Brazeway coil cooling your refrigerator.)

In 2008 and 2009, Brazeway experienced the same economic difficulties as many other manufacturing companies. "In a two-year period," says Stephanie, "we saw our combined industry cut almost in half." But in late 2007, just before the coming economic crash, they made the painful decision to close their hometown plant in Adrian, Michigan, and transfer the business to another plant. Many of these workers had been with the plant for decades; some had parents and grandparents who'd worked there. Having grown up in Adrian, Stephanie had known these people for most of her life. She had gone to school with many of them.

"Once we made the decision to close the plant," says Stephanie, "my team and I decided to announce it immediately, and I told them I had to be the one to do it."

This went counter to a recommendation Stephanie had received from lawyers that they delay making the announcement until just before the actual closure took place, which was not to be for another nine months. "We were warned that once our people knew the plant was closing," says Stephanie, "they might slack off in their production or even tamper with the equipment."

Stephanie and her team didn't buy it.

"At Brazeway, respect is paramount among our principles," she says. "We believe you have to deliver bad news in an honest and timely way. Ambiguity will cripple an organization. We needed to respect that these families needed time to plan for their future."

Another recommendation Stephanie ignored was the advice to hire security forces to deal with the angry reactions they were sure to have. "Doing this would have undermined trust," says Stephanie, "so we took the risk—and we got none of that reaction." Instead, what happened proved to be an experience that, if anything, brought the community closer together.

"I made the announcement together with a woman who was then our plant manager. We knew it would be hard on both of us," recalls Stephanie. "Especially as women, we often feel the need to be perceived as strong. But in this case, I told her, 'Don't cover up your emotions. Be yourself and show them you care.'"

They made the announcement personally to all three shifts at the plant, letting them know exactly what was happening and why, and how it was the only possible avenue to keep the company from losing the business, as the customer base had moved south.

"It was very emotional," says Stephanie. "I never thought we would close our hometown plant. I had to stop several times during the presentation to regain my composure. I'm sure they were angry and upset, but they didn't show it—perhaps because they could see how upset *I* was, too. At the end of our presentation, a group came up to me and said, 'Stephanie, we'll be okay—but will *you* be okay?' It was incredible."

But the greatest leadership lesson learned, says Stephanie, came from her plant manager. An employee approached her on the floor a week after the meeting and said, "I wish you had shown us how much you cared a long time ago." "When she shared that story with me," says Stephanie, "she paused and then added that this had changed her outlook as a manager forever."

In order to assist the employees during the closure, the company created severance packages and brought in an outside job-placement firm to offer guidance and help their people find new employment. They hoped the nine-month time frame would be helpful and give people time to adjust to this change in their lives.

"Many have told us how helpful all this was. I still try to keep in touch and help out where I can. You don't stop caring about people just because they don't work for you anymore."

In 2008 and 2009, as economic conditions continued hitting housing and automotive hard, Brazeway made another difficult but necessary decision in response to what they saw coming: they cut salaried staff at company headquarters by 30 percent. Just as with the plant closing the year before, it was Stephanie and her executive team who broke the news, meeting one-on-one with each affected staff member and their direct supervisor in their offices (*without* HR). When this process was over, Stephanie immediately convened a company-wide meeting, bringing the other plants in by teleconference to talk about what happened and why.

"Everyone in this room needs to understand that your job is safe, and we now need to focus on moving forward," she told them. During this meeting, she outlined the specific strategy, tactics, and plan to move the company forward.

"It was very interesting," she recalls. "The news was hard on everyone, and we all experienced the grief of losing good friends from the company. But despite this, we felt a rallying cry that day. There was a sense of mission and urgency that was beyond anything I'd ever experienced before. Some of our quietest people became our best performers. Everyone stepped up to a new level of excellence."

Stephanie's next step was to meet one-on-one with the "survivors," which she did *outside* the office.

"For the next three weeks, I had breakfast, lunch, dinner, beer at the local tavern, whatever environment was best suited to make that person feel comfortable. We talked about what happened and I assured them that they were critical to the business. I didn't want them to wonder if they were next. I also wanted the opportunity to directly discuss their individual roles in our performance, so that they would understand how important their jobs were."

To ensure that every employee was informed and focused, they also took steps to improve their communication process and frequency of measurement. They wanted to make sure everyone stayed updated and aware of how the strategy was working, and would understand what adjustments might be needed along the way.

After the layoffs the market continued to decline throughout 2009, but by year's end, Brazeway had exceeded all performance and profit expectations, and by mid-2010 they were *up* 38 percent. They were able to turn themselves around in just one year, a turnaround that Stephanie credits to their relationship and trust with their people.

Brazeway could have been just one more casualty of the economic downturn. Instead, because of a company philosophy that shows their people they care, through truthful and timely communication, it remains today a healthy, vibrant, and growing company.

WHAT WE HAVE HERE IS A FAILURE TO COLLABORATE

A strong measure of the importance of collaboration is the problems that can easily occur when it is missing. The lack of collaboration can undermine the best of intentions and cause even your allies to begin working against you rather than with you. I saw a dramatic example of this during my time at the Kennedy School, during the Harvard presidency of Larry Summers.

Larry came to speak at the Kennedy School in early 2001, much to the excitement and anticipation of students, faculty, and administration alike. A brilliant economist and distinguished public servant, he had just finished eight years of service in the Clinton administration, most recently as secretary of the treasury. There was quite a bit of buzz that he was on the short list to become Harvard's new president, replacing the mild-mannered Renaissance literature scholar Neil Rudenstine.

I knew and admired Larry from my time in the White House. When he heard about my At the Table program, he had generously reached out to the Women's Office and let me know his willingness to participate in those events on his many travels. In fact, he was the first male political appointee to do so. Originally, we had thought of the program as being just for women appointees talking to women across the country—but Larry expanded my thinking.

As it turned out, the short-list buzz was accurate. Sure enough, a few months later my husband, Rob, and I were attending Larry Summers's inauguration ceremony in Cambridge. Next to the inauguration of a US president, the induction of a new president at Harvard, with its centuries of history and ritual, ranks among the most impressive ceremonies I've witnessed. This was coming full circle for Larry, who at twenty-eight had served as one of Harvard's youngest-ever tenured professors.

A few years later, in August of 2004, I sat next to Larry at a brunch held at the home of Mort Zuckerman, the owner of *U.S. News & World Report*. I turned to Larry at one point and asked, "From a leadership standpoint, what has surprised you most in your first few years as Harvard's president?"

"Well," he said, "I wanted to become a tenured faculty member myself because I didn't want a boss. And now that I'm the president, I have all these people who work for me who don't think they have a boss!"

It wasn't hard to understand his frustration. In a way, university presidents have all the responsibility and none of the authority. You can't fire tenured faculty (that's what *tenured* means), so the only way you can succeed is through creating coalitions of people who are willing to work with you to help move your agenda forward. This entails being willing to make room for different ideas and opinions (including those you may disagree with), and creating an environment where people feel heard, valued, and acknowledged.

However, Larry has a different style. With his piercing intellect and inquisitive nature he would probe and test an idea, exploring it to its fullest. That kind of challenging style can lead to more robust research and is often how new ideas and insights are born. This may have worked well in scholarly debate or policy discussions at the World Bank or the White House, but it is not the style needed to build consensus, and it did not work well for him in the context of university life. Instead of feeling challenged and stimulated, faculty and colleagues more often felt dismissed and embarrassed.

In a lunchtime talk at a conference in January 2005, Larry suggested that women's underrepresentation in the top levels of academia might be due in part to a "different availability of aptitude at the high end." He later defended his remarks, saying they were purely "an attempt at provocation," but they nevertheless spurred a wave of protest, and two months later members of the Harvard faculty met and passed a resolution of "lack of confidence." Within a year he announced his resignation.

Larry's remark about women scientists was not in itself something that would bring down a presidency, but the reaction to it was an indication that his reservoir of goodwill had been drained. As a brilliant economist, intellectual sparring was how he authentically engaged with his colleagues, but while it might have been academically stimulating, that approach worked against him in his role as a university president.

This was especially unfortunate because Larry Summers had a robust and impressive agenda for his presidency. His vision for the university included goals to reduce class size, support faculty excellence, expand the university's real estate, and increase student involvement. And the students loved him; in fact, the *Harvard Crimson* reported that the students opposed his resignation by a three-to-one margin. (At the time, my husband, Rob Keller, was the Harvard men's volleyball coach. President Summers was fascinated with volleyball, and the fact that he took the initiative and the time to come to one of their games was a highlight of the year for both the team and their coach.)

Yet with all these factors going for him, he was still unable to execute his long-term vision. Why? Not because of any lack of qualifications, brilliance, passion, or dedication to Harvard, but simply because his style of engagement did not foster effective collaboration.

A DIFFICULT RELATIONSHIP

Creating true collaboration isn't always easy. Sometimes it can be quite a task just to get to the place where working together is possible at all. I've certainly been in situations where I've experienced how challenging it can be to forge a good working partnership.

However, I've also seen how incredibly worthwhile it is to make the effort to do so.

When I joined the Center for Public Leadership in the fall of 2003, I entered what soon proved to be a difficult relationship. Just three years old at the time, the center was being led by David Gergen and its first executive director, Harvard faculty member Barbara Kellerman. After three years, Barbara had decided it was time for her to step down from this position and focus more of her time on teaching and research, and David recruited me from the alumni office to be her successor. However, Barbara was staying on at the center as director of research as well as a member of the faculty, and she had negotiated as part of her contract that she would report directly to David. It was not an easy transition from the start, and it led to a contentious relationship for my first year there.

There were a number of reasons for this. To begin with, my experience and expertise had been more in the world of politics and not in academia, which was Barbara's milieu. The author of many respected books on leadership (including *Leadership: Essential Selections on Power, Authority, and Influence,* and *Followership: How Followers Are Creating Change and Changing Leaders*), Barbara was a noted authority with thirty years of credentials in the field. I had a master's in public administration from the Kennedy School, but no PhD, which is the key credibility factor for a career in academia. What I did bring to the table was a fresh point of view from my recent experience as director of alumni, as well as having recently been a graduate student myself.

Barbara had worked hard those first three years to lay a solid academic foundation at the center, and she was quite invested in the direction they had created. I brought a very different background of practical experience in politics and government, along with all sorts of new ideas. During my time there, we took the center in a more student-focused direction that was centered around personal and interpersonal awareness. This manifested in a series of outside-the-classroom programs and study groups, student trips to DC (like the one where I had first met Barack Obama), and other new initiatives, such as the America's Best Leaders Project.

As Barbara put it recently, "We had different agendas for the center."

We did indeed. Barbara did not feel part of the new direction of the center and was annoyed by what she felt was my lack of appreciation for her years in the leadership field. For my part, I found her difficult and unsupportive. It was a recipe for disaster, and grew only more so over time. After a year it became painfully clear: we needed to do something to shift the relationship.

HITTING THE SAME GROOVE AND FLYING TOGETHER

We decided to meet to discuss the situation. The two of us sat together over lunch and began the painful task of putting a voice to the animosity that had grown between us.

We listened intently to each other's experiences and perceptions of the past year and began looking for common ground. Although we came at it from different perspectives, we realized that we both cared deeply about the center and its success. It was such a small operation within the Harvard universe, and still so new, it just didn't make sense to allow friction between us to get in the way. We each had experiences the other did not—and we clearly shared a passion for the field of leadership. In the words of Marshall Ganz, we each had *our own* story; now we needed to create a new story—the story of *us* and how we might work together for the betterment of the center we both cared about.

During that lunch, Barbara and I agreed that we would continue to meet regularly, just the two of us. And we did: for months afterward, we met for breakfast every two weeks. Over the course of these talks, we began to appreciate each other and feel a new sense of collegiality. Instead of a challenge or impediment to my role at the center, I came to see her as a resource to draw upon, a source of experience and wisdom. I began to seek her advice and counsel about various issues at the center, and found her academic and historical perspective incredibly beneficial. She, in turn, began feeling more respected and included in the life of the center.

As Barbara puts it, "It was helpful for us to get out of the roles we were in and get together in a more informal way, where we could recognize and appreciate each other's strengths."

This tactic does not always work. Some people are so committed to being right, or so married to their own perspective, that they won't bend enough to meet you halfway. Fortunately for Barbara and me, ours was a situation where it did work.

My time with Barbara reminds me of a passage I read recently, written by the famed guitarist and innovator Les Paul:

> There is nothing like the joy of jamming when everybody hits the same groove and flies together. It lifts you off the ground, and there is no other high like it. It's what you live for as a musician, and listening and paying attention to what the other guy is doing is essential to getting there. The sad thing is, it's so obvious, yet so few do it. And it's a terrible problem musi-

cally when a person just goes his way with blinders on, without listening to the whole sound.[1]

It would have been easy for Barbara and me to continue avoiding each other and never make the effort to "listen to the whole sound." Our willingness to bridge that gap and build a new relationship was good for each of us personally—and it was also good for the center.

In December 2008, after the Obama campaign was over, the Center for Public Leadership invited me back to the Kennedy School to talk with students about leadership lessons learned from the campaign. As I looked out into the audience, there was Barbara, sitting in the front row. In that moment, two things struck me: first, how impossible this would have seemed back in the fall of 2003; and second, how happy it made me to see her and call her my friend.

THREE WAYS TO HANDLE
DIFFICULT RELATIONSHIPS

As rewarding as it was for Barbara and me to find common ground, it's not realistic to expect that this will always be possible in every situation. Sometimes people just won't budge, and sometimes you can't find your way to a resolution no matter how hard you try.

When speaking with groups about leadership, I am often asked questions like these: "How do you deal with difficult or unkind

---

1. This is taken from an inscription on the wall of *Les Paul's House of Sound,* the Les Paul exhibit at Discovery World, the science and technology museum in Milwaukee.

people? What do you do when someone just doesn't like you, or someone you thought was your friend or ally, isn't?"

These are tough questions, and we've all been there.

When you find you're butting heads with someone or you are in what feels like a toxic relationship, from what I've seen there are only three possible paths to take.

First, try your best to *repair* it. What this usually takes is being willing to set your own viewpoints aside for the moment and make a genuine effort to see the other person's perspective, as well as their strengths, skills, experience, and values. You don't have to agree with the other person in order to be able to work together; you don't even necessarily have to like them. If you can find some sort of common goal you share, then you have a basis for working together effectively.

This is what Barbara and I did, and in time we discovered that we not only had common ground but we did in fact grow to respect each other and genuinely like each other as well. Sometimes all it takes is a simple acknowledgment that things have gotten off track, and a willingness to start fresh.

But again, this isn't always possible. Sometimes the other person has decided, for whatever reason, that they just aren't willing to collaborate with you. It could be for a myriad of reasons, from a simple misunderstanding or misperception to a personality clash. Maybe they heard something about you (accurate or not) that colored their thinking. Maybe they are hoping to get your job, and you are in the way. Maybe they're unhappy with their own life. It may have nothing whatsoever to do with you. It just is what it is. The reason is less important than what you choose to do about it.

I found myself in a situation like this while working at the Obama campaign headquarters. It was the first time I had encountered such hostility from someone in the workplace. I tried to fix the situation, but it was impossible—the door was closed.

If you can't repair or resolve the situation, then the second path is *deciding to live with it*. This means doing whatever it takes to work around the problem: creating alternative channels of communication, restructuring work flow, finding an advocate in the chain of command, whatever you have to do to cordon off the toxicity so it doesn't get in the way of your work or spill over to infect the larger organization. This also takes a certain level of emotional maturity, because it means accepting a fundamentally irresolvable conflict and choosing simply to work around it.

My friend Amy Millman helped me gain perspective on this. Amy and I worked together in the Clinton administration; since then she has been president of Springboard Enterprises, an organization that helps women entrepreneurs access venture capital. She is also part of my personal support system, and I had shared with her several times the frustration I was having trying to deal with this situation.

One day, Amy said to me, "Betsy, you have a thousand people in your life who love you—why are you obsessing about this one person who doesn't? It's not going to change! Let it go!"

She was so right. And from that point on, I made the decision to simply work around this conflict as best I could. I will always be grateful to Obama senior adviser Pete Rouse, who helped navigate around this situation and keep it from coloring all that was good and constructive about everything we were doing.

Still, sometimes even this strategy doesn't work: there may be times when we simply cannot work around or contain the problem. (For example, the circumstance I just described was only manageable because it was a short-term situation, and I could see the end in sight.) That leaves path number three, which is to *leave*. Whether this means resigning from a job, changing assignments, or letting go of a friendship, there are times in life when the most positive and sane thing we can do is make a clear decision to say good-bye.

I believe one of the most valuable insights we can have is the realization that we cannot change other people's behavior—we can only control how we respond. When things aren't working, we can try to fix it; we can stay and find ways to live with it; or we can walk away.

CLOSE BONDS ACROSS THE AISLE

A key ingredient in creating true collaboration is becoming aware of our assumptions and learning to challenge them. In fact, challenging our own assumptions can open us up to learning from people and situations we never thought possible, and can even sometimes lead to the unlikeliest of friendships.

In the fall of 1993, soon after arriving at my new post in the Clinton administration, I got a call one day from the office of Pete Domenici, the venerable Republican senator from New Mexico: the senator wanted to see me. I had just started working at the SBA as director of the Office of Women's Business Ownership, and my job included overseeing a national network of women's business centers that provided management and technical assistance to women who were small business owners. At the time, this was a fairly small program, with about $1 million in funding and ninety centers across the country, two of which happened to be in New Mexico. To my delight, Senator Domenici was a fan of the centers, and he wanted to meet the person who was going to be running them.

Soon after his call I went up the Hill to visit him in his office. Curious about his interest in the women's centers and his dedication to women's economic empowerment, I asked him about that.

"Well," he said, "I have six daughters, and they keep me in line." We both laughed, and I knew I'd found a friend.

Men who have daughters often have a different level of awareness and understanding of women and the issues they face, and there was no better example of this than Pete Domenici. He was a champion for this program and in his role as chairman of Appropriations, he was dedicated to seeing the program grow. Over the eight years of the Clinton administration, through the efforts of a bipartisan partnership, the program's funding increased from $1 million to $12 million. Our collaboration together is one of my fondest memories of that time.

As a Democrat, I had made the assumption that this lifelong Republican would not be that friendly to my ideas, that he and I would be on different sides of the fence. As it turned out, nothing could be further from the truth.

Another thing that touched me about Senator Domenici was the deep respect and friendship he shared with the late Senator Paul Wellstone, a Democrat from Minnesota. Their views were polar opposites on almost every issue—except one. Both men had had experience with mental illness in their families that connected them on a deep, personal level, and it was in their work together on mental health legislation that the two got past their ideological differences and formed a bond.

Senator Domenici once shared with me that, much to his surprise, Senator Wellstone had become one of his closest friends. "Can you believe it, Betsy?" he added. I could, because while they may have had clear differences in their views about policy and political philosophy, they understood this fact of humanity: there is far more we share in common than that which makes us different.

This was also true of the unlikely bond between Orrin Hatch and the late Ted Kennedy. Among the many tributes to Senator Kennedy that aired in the days following his passing in the summer of 2009, none was more moving than the interviews with Senator Hatch. Kennedy, the eastern liberal Democrat, and Hatch, the conservative Utah Republican, could not have disagreed more vehemently on nearly every issue they debated, and yet through the course of their years on the Senate floor together they forged a connection that started as mutual respect and grew to become a deep and genuine friendship. As Hatch put it:

> As a Republican coming from Utah, I stated many times on the campaign trail that I planned to come to Washington to fight Ted Kennedy. When I came to Washington, I hadn't the slightest idea that I would eventually have a strong working relationship with and love for the man that I came to fight. If you had told me that he would have become one of my closest friends in the world, I probably would have suggested that you needed professional help. But that's exactly what happened.[2]

For almost two decades, Hatch and Kennedy alternated as chairman and ranking member of the Senate Labor Committee.[3] During that time they worked together to craft some of the nation's

---

2. CBS News, August 28, 2009.

3. This committee has now been renamed Committee on Health, Education, Labor and Pensions (HELP).

most important health legislation, including the Dietary Supplement Health and Education Act and a dozen other major bills.[4] It is an amazing legislative record—and a testament to what can happen when people are willing to collaborate.

Ironically, the bill that Senators Domenici and Wellstone collaborated on, the Paul Wellstone and Pete Domenici Mental Health Parity and Addiction Equity Act of 2008 (which requires insurance companies to treat mental health on an equal basis with physical illnesses), passed into law during Pete Domenici's final year in Congress, twelve years after being introduced and six years after Senator Wellstone's death—and only with the support of a Democratic senator from Massachusetts: Ted Kennedy.

MY REPUBLICAN TEACHERS

I learned a big lesson about friendships across the aisle during my time as a grad student at Harvard.

---

4. This history of legislative collaboration includes passage of: the Orphan Drug Act, which provided tax credits for encouraging the development of medicines for rare diseases; the Ryan White AIDS act, which established a federally funded program for people living with HIV/AIDS; the State Children's Health Insurance Program (SCHIP), which provided health insurance to thousands of the working poor across the nation; the Mammography Quality Standards in 1992; the Americans with Disabilities Act; the FDA Revitalization Act of 2007, which addressed many critical issues concerning the safety of pharmaceuticals and medical devices; PDUFA, a program that created drug user fees to help expedite the approval of new drugs; the Health Centers Renewal Act of 2007, which reauthorized the health center program and provided people with essential health-care services; the FDA Modernization Act of 1997, which regulated prescription drug advertising and codified the requirements for access to lifesaving medicines; Bioshield legislation, increasing federal, state, and local infrastructure for bioterrorism preparedness; and the Serve America Act, which renewed America's call for volunteer service to meet some of our country's most challenging problems and needs.

When a new administration takes office in Washington, many
of those who worked in the previous administration find themselves in academia. When I arrived at Harvard to work on my
master's degree, there was still a year and a half to go in President
Clinton's second term, which meant that some of the most interesting people on campus were Republicans (interestingly, all with
White House experience). Although I've had a strong Democratic
affiliation all my life, I have always welcomed both Democrats and
Republicans as friends and mentors. It's interesting to hear how
others with different opinions think about an issue. Neither party
has all the answers.

That first semester, three of my four classes were with Republican faculty members: Roger Porter, who had been a top economic
and domestic policy adviser for George H. W. Bush and Ronald
Reagan; David Gergen, who worked for three Republican administrations before going to work for President Clinton as communications director; and Dick Darman.

Darman had an extraordinarily rich résumé of White House
experiences. He had held positions under five presidents, as deputy
director of treasury, budget director, deputy chief of staff, and a
slew of other roles. He was most famously director of the Office of
Management and Budget under George H. W. Bush and the person responsible for the "Read my lips: no new taxes" line. As one
of Reagan's closest advisers, he was also credited as the source behind the proposed "ketchup as a vegetable" USDA directive. Brilliant and tireless, he could also be brusque and rankle those who
disagreed with his ideas. At the same time, his willingness to work
with Democrats was well known and annoyed some conservatives.

I first signed up for Darman's class because I was intrigued
with his extensive Washington résumé and his ideology. What kind

of person would classify ketchup as a vegetable? I fully anticipated that I would not like him as a person. Much to my surprise, the situation proved to be quite the opposite.

During that semester I took every opportunity to hear more about my professors' experiences in Washington. Several times a semester, instructors would create opportunities for students to meet informally outside of class. I attended a number of these gatherings and loved hearing Darman's stories and insights. He was engaging and had a great sense of humor—and a huge heart. I found him fascinating.

It would have been easy to approach my year at Harvard by seeking out only those professors who shared my Democratic perspectives and political leanings. Yet if I had, how much less would I have ended up learning there? Who would have thought that so much of what I took from that year—not only the academic learning, but also the enrichment of personal insights, life wisdom, and new friendships—would have come from teachers who were staunch Republicans? Yet that is exactly what happened, and if I had not been willing to hear and learn from people who held political points of view very different from my own, I would have missed out on so many enriching experiences.

A RICHER LIFE

One thing that especially drew me to Dick Darman was his obvious affection for his mentor, Elliot Richardson. Sometimes jokingly referred to by his friends as "the former everything" because of all the major posts he held in government, Richardson had served in four different positions as cabinet secretary, more than anyone else in US history. He also served as ambassador to the Court of St. James (that is, to Britain, the most prestigious American ambassadorial post there is), negotiated the worldwide treaty on the Law of the Sea, and was the chief representative of the United Nations in monitoring Nicaraguan elections in 1990, among other assignments.[5] In many of these positions, Darman had worked for him.

The two of us talked a lot about Secretary Richardson that semester at Harvard. I was always curious about him and his influence on Darman's career and asked a lot of questions. I had always admired Richardson for his principled stand during the Watergate affair, when, as Richard Nixon's attorney general, he refused to fire special prosecutor Archibald Cox, a decision that cost him his job—and earned him a special place in the nation's history. A quarter century later, in 1998, Secretary Richardson was awarded the Presidential Medal of Freedom, the nation's highest civilian honor.

In December 1999, near the end of my first semester at Harvard, Dick Darman brought in Elliot Richardson as guest lecturer for his class on Strategic Management in the Public Sector. The classroom, Land Hall, is on the fifth floor of the Belfer Building. Almost eighty and with his health declining, he refused to take the elevator, and insisted on walking up the five flights.

He was a handsome, elegant man and looked very dapper in his chocolate-brown suit. He sat with the class for the full ninety minutes, sharing his lessons of management and leadership. It was somewhat difficult to understand him. He had suffered a stroke and

---

5. It was Richardson's role as chief monitor in the elections through which Nicaraguans voted out the corrupt Sandinista government that gave those elections international credibility.

lost some of his capacity for language, but it was crystal clear that he had not lost any of his passion for public service.

Equally clear was Darman's respect for his mentor. He sat quietly next to him and did not try to intercede or interpret.

We were in awe of Richardson's vast leadership experiences in the public sector. One student asked, "Mr. Secretary, of everything you've done in your illustrious career, what are you most proud of?"

We had to listen carefully to understand his reply; nobody wanted to miss a syllable or a nuance. You could have heard a pin drop. Secretary Richardson leaned forward, speaking each word with care. "Everything I have accomplished," he said, "pales in comparison to what I have left undone."

It was the truest, most poignant definition of what public service is about, and was what every one of us in that class was there to learn.

After class I went to the podium to meet him. Darman introduced me and shared the fact that I had just come from the Clinton administration. Richardson grabbed me by both shoulders, looked at me with a smile, and said, "When are you going to run for office?" We chatted for a moment until another student engaged him. As I turned to leave, my eyes filled with tears. I looked over at Darman and we exchanged a glance that acknowledged the depth and impact of the moment.

Elliot Richardson died two weeks later, on New Year's Eve 1999, leaving us with an example of genuine leadership for the new century ahead.

My encounter with Elliot Richardson was one of the high points of my academic career—and it would never have happened if I had not let myself develop a friendship with this curmudgeonly Republican teacher.

When you open yourself to people who are different from you, sometimes it leads to beautiful surprises and can make life so much richer.

Here is how Georgette Mosbacher puts it:

> There's not enough civility today among people with different points of view, let alone camaraderie. We don't have to agree on everything, yet we can still like and respect each other. We can say, "Hey, there's another point of view—okay, let me hear yours." And who knows? I've come full circle on a lot of things in my life.
>
> Too many people start out with preconceived ideas, and they decide they don't like you before they even know you. And that's dangerous. That's how you become a zealot. If you aren't willing to hear another point of view, how do you grow?

Georgette is another example of an unlikely friendship. We first met when I invited Georgette to sit on the board of the Center for Public Leadership, as part of my effort to increase Republican representation there. During the 2008 election season, Georgette served as cochair of John McCain's presidential campaign. I would call her occasionally, and despite the fact that we were working for opposing campaigns, she was a great support for me and it always felt like we were kindred spirits.

Georgette and I have very different points of view on many things—and yet we are good friends. Her wisdom and perspective on the political and social issues of the day continue to broaden my thinking and understanding.

How to Take the Lead

The old command-and-control style of leadership said, "I know what needs to be done, so do what I say." The new model of leadership understands that no man or woman is an island, and that we rarely get anything significant done on our own. Genuine accomplishment is the product of teamwork, not the lone feat of a single unaided hero.

- Do you seek out points of view that are significantly different from your own? Some of our best strategies and life lessons come from those who see things quite differently from the way we do.

- To create the most effective collaboration, consider these three steps:
  1. Listen to all the available perspectives.
  2. Then, based on the insights gleaned, take decisive action.
  3. Finally, clearly communicate your decisions, including why you made them and what they mean, to the team.

- Do you consistently keep your team informed, even when the news is bad or problems comes up? It's easy to communicate only the good news, but it's crucial to include your people in the process no matter what. When times are tough and difficult decisions need to be made, let your people know in an honest and timely way.

- How do you handle a difficult relationship at work? When faced with a conflict or challenging relationship in the workplace, consider these three possible paths:
  1. Try your best to repair it. Set your own viewpoints aside and make a genuine effort to see the other person's perspective. See if you can find some shared goal or common ground.

2. Decide to live with it. If you can't repair it, do whatever it takes to work around it. Create alternative channels of communication, restructure work flow, find an advocate in the chain of command, cordon off the toxicity.

3. Let go and make a clear decision to say good-bye. Whether this means resigning from a job, changing assignments, or letting go of a friendship, sometimes the most positive step is to move on.

- Whom do you know who has views substantially different from yours? If all your friends and colleagues have the same opinions you do, you're probably missing out on some valuable insight. Often our greatest friendships, alliances, and life experiences come from our association with people quite unlike ourselves.

6. LEARNING

Uncontaminated Curiosity

On January 15, 2009, I was in the ER with my husband, who had torn his Achilles tendon playing basketball and needed immediate attention. The television in the room where we sat together while he was being prepped for surgery was tuned to CNN. Eyes glued to the television, our own medical emergency suddenly forgotten, we sat riveted by the unfolding story of a US Airways plane that had just made an emergency landing in the Hudson River.

Steeling ourselves to hear awful news of a terrible tragedy, we instead saw images of passengers standing alive and well, huddled on the wing of the waterlogged plane and awaiting rescue. Because of the actions of the pilot and his crew, not a single life had been lost. The pilot's split-second decision to land the aircraft in the river and his flawless execution of that difficult maneuver had saved not only those 155 people but countless others whose lives would have been endangered had he chosen the alternative course of attempting to return to the airport—a choice that would likely have resulted in a crash landing in the middle of Manhattan.

Having grown up with a dad who was a pilot, I found myself extremely curious to know more about this man, his thoughts about the incident and about what made it possible to step so immediately into the role of a leader when the stakes were so high. Ten months later, sitting in a crowded ballroom surrounded by 1,500 people, I had that very opportunity, when I heard Captain Chesley "Sully" Sullenberger speak at Elliott Masie's annual learning conference in November in Orlando, Florida.

When Sully was introduced and walked out onto the stage, the entire ballroom stood up and gave him a standing ovation. The outpouring of respect, gratitude, and goodwill that filled the room was palpable. Many (including me) had tears in their eyes.

Captain Sullenberger is a humble man, and this all seemed to make him a bit uncomfortable. Elliott Masie, an expert in leadership and technology, proceeded to interview Sully about the incident itself, and also about how his life had brought him to that point and what lessons people might take away from his life and leadership.

"I have been very fortunate," said Sully. "First, to have found my passion early in life. I knew at the age of five that I was going to be a pilot, and have been lucky enough to be able to do this my entire life. This gave me a great advantage; it allowed me to work very hard and become an expert in something that I loved and cared about. My curiosity fueled my lifelong learning."

He talked about how that passion for learning had ensured that he never lost mastery of the plane. At Purdue he pursued an accelerated master's program that combined human factors science (essentially, ergonomics as applied to aviation) and cognitive psychology. In addition to being a pilot, he ran his own safety consulting business and helped develop the crew resource management course taught by US Airways. As planes became more and more sophisticated, he made an effort to keep learning, making sure that no matter how far automation and technological innovation pushed the envelope, he was keeping up in his own skill set as well as his grasp of the latest designs and features. For forty years of careful practice and training, he never stopped in his pursuit of excellence as a pilot.

When crisis erupted on that cold January day, there could not have been anyone more fully prepared than Chesley Sullenberger. A lifetime of learning came together in one leadership moment, lasting less than four minutes, that changed the lives of 155 people and their families and inspired the nation. His entire career had served to prepare him for those 208 seconds.

MASTER YOUR AREA

Talking with Warren Bennis recently about his life and accomplishments, I asked him to what he attributed his prominence in the leadership field.

"There are three key factors," he replied. "The capacity to engage others—which is all about listening. Second, hard work and discipline: the determination to keep at it and keep showing up. And finally, *uncontaminated curiosity*. I keep wanting to know more."

Another person who has that trait of uncontaminated curiosity is Donna Shalala, who was President Clinton's secretary of Health and Human Services throughout his eight years in office. Secretary Shalala has a passion for learning, and whatever area she is working in at the time, she always takes care to thoroughly *know the material*.

During that intense time in the summer of 1996 surrounding President Clinton's signing of the welfare reform bill, Donna appeared before an audience at the American Sociological Association to defend the legislation.

"It was a very lively session," she recalls with gracious understatement. "I took on some of the biggest sociologists in the country, and they were hot under the collar. A few of them actually got to their feet as they talked. Many of these people were poverty experts who had studied welfare for years, and were convinced that this bill was the end of the world. They were loaded for bear—but they had not carefully read the entire bill. I had."

In fact, Donna had also been engaged in this issue for years. While serving as president of Hunter College in New York, she had been on New York Governor Mario Cuomo's welfare reform task force, and she knew exactly how welfare worked and why it needed reform. What's more, she knew the bill backward and forward.

"In the end," she says, "I won their respect, because I understood the material."

Effective leaders are always pushing the envelope of their knowledge and mastery of their area. Eleanor Roosevelt once said, "I think, at a child's birth, if a mother could ask a fairy godmother to endow it with the most useful gift, that gift should be curiosity." Chesley Sullenberger, Warren Bennis, and Donna Shalala all share that particular gift—and are at the top of their fields.

KEEPING A DOOR ALWAYS OPEN TO LEARNING

It's easy to become complacent, to reach certain levels in our career where our learning becomes stagnant. But the world never stands still, and there are always new things to learn. Leaders never stop challenging themselves and pushing themselves to learn more. Their uncontaminated curiosity, as Warren Bennis put it, keeps them at the top of their game.

Another person in the Clinton administration who had a remarkable ability to embrace learning was James Lee Witt, head of the Federal Emergency Management Agency (FEMA). Witt had worked as state emergency management director for Clinton when he was governor of Arkansas, and when the president took office in the White House with a commitment to clean up and strengthen FEMA, he tapped the man he knew could do the job. Witt had his work cut out for him. A report on the agency by Congress the year before had described it this way: "FEMA is widely viewed as a political dumping ground—a turkey farm, if you will, where large numbers of positions exist that can be conveniently and quietly filled by political appointment . . ." [1]

As with the SBA, the president elevated the director of FEMA to the level of a cabinet position and, just as with Erskine Bowles and the SBA, it was James Lee Witt who reversed the agency's poor reputation.

One of his first actions at the agency was to call in the top ten senior career civil servants and inform them that they were all going to switch jobs for one year. When they objected vigorously, he told them, "Listen, if you're not happy with this arrangement three months from now, we can change. Meanwhile my door is always open." (He confided to me once that his open-door policy was part of how he liked to manage, creating times in the schedule specifically for people in the agency at all levels to visit with him

---

1. Bill Gertz, "Mikulski Faults FEMA Officials, Calls for Probe," *Washington Times*, September 4, 1992.

and share their ideas and concerns.) When the three months had elapsed, not a single one of the ten came looking for their old position back.

It's so easy to get stuck in our perspective and stop seeing new opportunities, viewpoints, and possibilities. James Lee Witt knew that in order for the agency to change and grow, the senior people there had to see the agency from a different perspective. They had to let go of their assumptions and start learning again.

My friend John Whitmore, who worked as my deputy at the SBA when I was director of entrepreneurial development there, spent the majority of his career at the SBA, holding posts that included budget director and acting administrator. John once shared with me the observation, based on his career of more than twenty years, that people often held jobs for longer than they probably should. "After three years in the same position," he said, "people often become less effective. As they grow more comfortable in the job, it is easy to become more complacent and stop learning."

GET OUTSIDE YOUR BUBBLE

One way leaders learn is to get outside the bubble of their own experience or comfort zone and discover what is happening in the lives of people around them. Nobody is more committed to doing this than Donna Shalala. At the University of Miami, where she is currently president, Donna teaches a course on the US health-care system. In her course she tells her students:

"If you know only the experience of people who grew up in Ivy League homes, this is a disaster for policy. You *have* to make time to sit down and learn about people's lives from different perspectives. Ask everyone who provides a service for you what their health care is like. Ask the guy at the gas station, at the dry cleaner's, at the grocery store. Get their stories so you can understand the variety of people's experiences."

As a university president, this is exactly what she does. Like Peter Ueberroth, Donna believes in "management by walking around." She drives around the campus and drops in on students and faculty just to visit and check in with them. When she was president of the University of Wisconsin, she would do the same thing. In her desire to stay connected to students and university life outside the classroom, she was known for visiting the fraternities and sororities on Saturday nights, and the students loved her.

Secretary Shalala shared with me that the proudest moments in her career have been times when she was able to help individual people take advantage of opportunities and get on with their lives. As an example, she told me a story from her days as president of Hunter College. A friend who worked at a nonprofit called to tell Donna about a young man who did some cleaning in her office. "We have to lay him off," her friend said. "Do you think you might have anything for him on the cleaning staff there at Hunter?"

"We might," said Donna. "Send him up to talk to me."

"I will," the friend said. "Oh, and I should mention that he's illiterate, so he really can't fill out any job applications or anything like that."

The next day, the young man showed up at Donna's office. He was about twenty years old, and the first thing she asked him was why he could not read.

"How did that happen?" she said.

"When I was a kid," he replied, "my mother was an alcoholic. I went to school one day wearing torn, dirty jeans, and they sent me home. I just never went back."

Since then, he'd done a series of odd jobs to support himself, most recently being on the cleaning staff at Donna's friend's office. The friend was simply hoping to help the young man get another cleaning job—but Donna saw something in him, a willingness to learn and to step up, that prompted her to go further.

There was a program at Hunter for freshmen who had not completed their high school education. Donna managed to get the young man into that program, and not only did he learn to read and write but he also went on to complete his college education—and today he is a supervisor at Hunter College.

"It was very hard," says Donna, "but it changed his life."

"I'm very proud of what we did in the White House on welfare reform," she adds, "and children's insurance, and other big programs. But I am even prouder of helping individuals like that young man to open up new opportunities and move their lives forward."

And the only reason it happened was that Donna was willing to pay attention, to step outside her own experience and learn about another person's situation. This has been a key aspect of Donna's leadership in every position she has held. As she says, "You have to make time in your schedule to listen and understand the community. That's where you learn."

AN ATMOSPHERE WHERE IT'S SAFE
TO TELL THE TRUTH

Effective leaders believe that their people have valuable perspectives, insights, and information. Because they are on the front lines, working with customers and constituents, they know at first hand what is working and what is not. So often, the answers are right there within our own teams or organizations—provided we are willing to listen and people feel safe enough to tell us.

One reason my time at the White House was so rewarding was the fact that President Clinton created an atmosphere where I was not afraid to tell him what I thought.

On June 20, 1996, just two months before the Democratic Convention and the heart of reelection campaign season, the president was scheduled to attend an annual luncheon held by the Women's Legal Defense Fund. Alexis Herman and I were driving with him to the event when he turned to us and said, "Did you see the campaign ad on the progress we've made on domestic violence?"

I had seen the ad—and the truth was, I found it upsetting because it missed the full scope of the issue. All the women featured in the ad were poor and black.

I said, "Yes, I've seen the ad . . . but honestly, Mr. President, I didn't like it."

"Really?!" He asked me to explain.

"Well, to begin with, domestic violence is not an issue that only impacts women who are poor and black. It's an *everyone* issue. One in four women—of all colors and nationalities—has experienced some form of domestic violence at least once."

I reminded him about the women whose stories we had heard at that October domestic violence awareness event the previous year. One of them was a professional woman who was married to a doctor and also earned a solid six figures in her own career. At a dinner party one night, right in front of their friends, her husband threw her down the stairs. Yet she continued to stay with him. It was only when he started going after their children that she finally took them and left. She was not in any way underprivileged or socioeconomically marginalized—but she was just as much the victim of domestic violence as anyone featured in that ad.

"Often," I said, "a woman stays with her abuser because she has so few economic options. But this woman had ample financial resources—and she *still* stayed. Mr. President, the problem with the ad is that it misrepresents the scope of the issue. It is so much more pervasive than being just a poor women's issue."

The president nodded. He didn't say much in response, but I knew him well enough to know that he was taking it in, as he always did.

Soon we arrived at the luncheon, and when the time came, he stood up to give his remarks. The speech touched on the array of policies and programs the administration had already implemented or was now working on to better the lives of women, children, and families. When he came to the issue of domestic violence, he said:

> I also want to say that we have more to do in the area of public safety, especially on the issue of domestic violence. A lot of you were particularly active when we were working for the Crime Bill in passing the Violence Against Women provisions and setting up the domestic violence operation in the Justice Department, which Bonnie Campbell is doing such a good job of heading. And I thank you for that.
>
> But there is more to be done there. Violence against women is certainly no stranger in this country. It is an unwelcome intruder.
>
> *And it is not a family problem, and it is not a woman problem, and let me say it is most assuredly not just a poor person's problem. This is an* American *problem that we have to face.*

At that, the audience erupted in applause—and I smiled to myself, because in addition to his prepared remarks, the president had just spontaneously added the last two sentences. This had happened only because, knowing he would listen, I was willing to tell him the truth as I saw it.

DEVELOPING A PERSONAL ADVISORY BOARD

My friend Elliott Masie, the founder of the MASIE Center, is one of the world's foremost experts on learning and knowledge in the workplace. Elliott suggests that every leader should be willing to sit down with his or her team once a month to ask them key learning questions: "What are we doing right, and what are we doing wrong?" And, if you're really courageous: "What behaviors am I doing that need to change?"

This is such a powerful thing to do, because none of us has all the answers or knows everything we need to know. I've always made it a point to surround myself with people who can give me that perspective and tell me the truth. In fact, in every organization where I have had a leadership role, I have always developed a *personal advisory board* as a key part of my strategy.

A personal advisory board is simply an informal group that serves to educate, support, and give us historical perspective—our own board of advisers to keep us connected to real-world issues and aspects of our work that we might not see otherwise. It also provides key relationships or opportunities that can help us keep an ear to the ground and stay connected to the constituencies we are there to serve.

At the SBA, I hosted a one-day strategy session with the former heads of the Office of Women's Business Ownership, both Republicans and Democrats. The former directors were more than happy to participate and felt good about being asked. During that session they shared their experiences with programs that had been successful and those that hadn't, and they helped me understand who were the key players at the agency and who on the Hill could be helpful. The insights gained from that one day saved me months of trying to avoid land mines and get up to speed on my own. This group became my informal advisers. Lindsey Johnson, my immediate predecessor in the George H. W. Bush administration, was especially invested in the work of the office and in seeing us build on the good work she'd done there. She became a particularly valuable adviser to me as well as a lifelong friend.

I did something similar when I went to the White House as director of the Women's Office. Because this office was newly created, in this case there were no former directors to call on, so I assembled an informal group of women political appointees from across the federal agencies, and we met in the Women's Office every two weeks for coffee and bagels. This group was instrumental in educating me about the policies, programs, and opportunities for women within their agencies. It's easy for White House staff to become isolated, and I knew that a key factor in my effectiveness in this new role would be my ability to stay connected and informed. This group became my eyes and ears, and I in turn was able to support their issues and ideas for presidential events.

In some cases you may find an advisory group already in place when you start at a position. This was true for me in my role as Kennedy School alumni director, where an alumni leadership board already existed, consisting of eight people elected from the alumni body. This group was helpful in setting the strategic mission of the office, and I spent time getting to know the individual board members and their goals and perspectives.

Sometimes an advisory board can be more personal. There is a small group of women I am part of who first came together around the discovery that we were all born the same summer of the same year. We began getting together each year simply to celebrate our birthdays, but we have since grown to become dear friends, and our group has morphed into a personal support system.

There's no right way or wrong way to develop a personal advisory board. We all have different needs at different times. But the bottom line is to ensure that we have the people in our life we can count on to give us a perspective we wouldn't have had on our own.

Which brings us to the all-important subject of *mentors.*

LEADERS ARE MENTORS

A mentor is a special kind of personal adviser, someone who brings out our most productive feelings and qualities by the way they support, nurture, guide, and acknowledge us. Being the kind of leader we've been exploring in this book *is* being a mentor. Mentorship is the essence of effective leadership, and mentoring people within an organization is a key element in the engagement and retention of top talent in today's workplace.

Hewitt Associates, a leading provider of human resources outsourcing and consulting, recently conducted a fascinating study to help understand what motivates top talent to deliver their best. They looked at seven Fortune 500 companies across a range of industries, collecting data from nearly 750 respondents. One of the most intriguing findings was that today's high performers don't simply want to be managed; they want to be *mentored*.

"For many athletes and artists, their success is greatly dependent on an inspirational coach, mentor, or muse. These individuals rely on the guidance of this leader to teach, reward, inspire, and grow. It's no different in the world of business."[2]

The Hewitt study identifies what they describe as a *relationship gap* between how managers rate their own performance as mentors, and how the high-performing employees they manage rate them. Nearly three-quarters of the managers (74 percent) believed they provided the support (feedback, coaching, etc.) the star employees needed to succeed at their jobs. Fewer than half the employees (49 percent) agreed. Nearly three-quarters of the managers (73 percent) believed they were helping their star employees to reach their goals, yet only 45 percent of those high-performing employees felt the same way. When asked if the managers were providing "important guidance on development opportunities," the question received a yes vote from nearly two-thirds of the managers (66 percent)—and from barely one-third of the employees (35 percent).

What this discrepancy really describes is not just a relationship gap but a *mentoring gap*. When people are mentored they feel cared about. It seems so simple—but it is a key driver to employee satisfaction and engagement in the workplace.

"Top talent is a company's greatest competitive weapon," say the report's authors. "To prevent their departure . . . managers

---

2. Nidhi Verma, Shelli Greenslade, and Mary Ann Armatys, "The Relationship Factor: How Satisfied Are High Potentials with Their Managers' Efforts to Manage and Develop Them?" *Align Journal*, May/June 2007.

should take personal responsibility to guide, develop, and grow their top talent into future leaders. Organizations, for their part, must develop 'people/relationship' managers."

Much of what I've been able to accomplish in my life has been due to the mentors I've been fortunate enough to have. From Hugh Beaton, my fifth-grade teacher, to Des Lizotte, my mentor in the life insurance and financial services business, to Warren Bennis at the Center for Public Leadership, in every situation where I've been at my best and most productive, there have been caring, generous people who took a personal interest in me and helped to pull the best out of me.

One of my most important mentors in the last few years has been Elliott Masie. In the summer of 2008, Elliott came to visit the Obama campaign headquarters and we spent an hour together. Although we had met before, we didn't really know each other. That hour of conversation would prove to have a significant impact on the direction my career would take after the campaign was over.

As we talked, I told him about the work I'd done at the Center for Public Leadership, and the thoughts and observations I'd been having about leadership on the campaign trail. At one point he said, "You know, Betsy, you should really consider stepping back into the leadership field. We need someone like you in the field, someone with a fresh voice, and especially a woman's voice."

After that visit, he called me every month just to check in. He would ask me what I was thinking and doing, and how he could support me. After the campaign was over, he offered me a contract to do some work on these leadership ideas with the MASIE Center, and then invited me to come speak at his learning conference— that same conference where I heard Chesley Sullenberger speak.

Elliott saw something in me that I didn't see in myself, and took a personal interest in helping me navigate a new direction in my career. He has introduced me to key people in the leadership field and given me valuable opportunities to explore these ideas. Even more importantly, he gave me the confidence in myself to pursue a new and uncharted chapter in my life.

A WARM BLANKET OF SUPPORT

A mentor is someone who sees our greatest qualities, who tells us the truth, who believes in us and brings out our most productive feelings. Mentors provide strength when we feel lost, help us see new opportunities, give us new perspectives on challenging situations, and provide the warm blanket of support to face the difficult moments in life. They celebrate our successes and are our biggest fans.

I saw a sweet example of this when I visited my sister Dee Dee and her family in February 2009, with my daughter, Madison, who was then six and a half years old. Dee Dee and her husband, Todd Purdum, had invited some friends over, and while the adults were sitting in the living room talking, the kids sat around a table to eat dinner. There were a few other kids there, including Dee Dee's nine-year-old daughter, Kate. Madison adores Kate and thinks of her as a big sister.

As the kids began eating, some of the boys, who had never met Madison before, decided she had a funny name and started to tease her, calling her "Dinglefloop." (How you get Dinglefloop from Madison I don't know, but questions of linguistic logic never stopped an eight-year-old boy.) Suddenly I realized that Madison had bolted from the table and was running upstairs, crying.

I followed her upstairs to find out what happened and try to console her. I was making little progress when Kate walked in. Kate is smart, a voracious reader, and has a strong personality with a mind of her own. Facing us with both hands on her hips, she said, "Madison, you cannot let *anyone* ruin your night. Tell you what else, those boys think they're so smart, but they're not: they can't even *spell* dinglefloop. And Madison, never *ever* let a boy make you cry. You can't let *anyone* do that."

She reached out for Madison's hand and said, "Come on downstairs with me."

Madison took Kate's hand and headed downstairs to face the boys.

Later I told Kate how proud I was of how she supported Madison. "If you keep up that confident attitude as you go through life, you are going to have one incredible journey," I said.

"Aunt Betsy," she replied, "you can never let anyone make you feel you're not as special as you are."

Kate gave her cousin a new way of looking at her situation. She gave her the support and confidence she needed to regain her composure that evening. She showed Madison her *own* strength, in a moment when Madison couldn't see it herself.

There's a word for what Kate did for Madison: she *mentored* her.

MENTORING CAN CHANGE A PERSON'S LIFE

It is amazing sometimes just how much impact mentoring can have. One of my favorite examples of someone who has changed her life with the help of mentors is Sava Berhané (pronounced *ber-hahn-AY*).

When I first met Sava, in October 2007, she was volunteering at Obama campaign headquarters as an intern in policy and helping with political outreach to minority women. She was just twenty-three years old.

Sava sought me out, asking a colleague to make an introduction because she had read something I'd written in *Newsweek* about leadership, and she wanted to share her reaction. The article was headlined "What I Learned," and it consisted of short pieces by ten women who had, in the editors' words, "found their own ways of overcoming obstacles."

Sava had certainly overcome many obstacles in her life. Growing up in Roxbury, one of Boston's poorest and roughest neighborhoods, at one point she and her mom and two sisters were living under the poverty line. Sava, although an engaged student, dropped out of high school for a year to help support the family. Yet she did not stop aspiring to reach her goals. With the intervention and assistance of several mentors, she was nominated as a McDonald's All-American athlete in high school basketball, and attended Mount Holyoke, a private girls' college in central Massachusetts, and then Oxford. Speaking of these mentors, she says, "They saw me, they affirmed me, and they brought out the best in me."

Her decision to join the Obama campaign was not an easy one; in fact, just making the trip from Boston to Chicago was challenging. She had just enough money saved to buy a ticket to Chicago. Before she arrived, a Mount Holyoke alum who lived in Chicago had offered to let Sava stay with her. "She lived near enough to headquarters," Sava explained, "that I could walk there every morning in a half hour and not have to worry about train money."

Sava and I clicked right away. A few weeks after we met, Sava came to me with a dilemma. The campaign had approached her about taking the position of acting state field director in Alabama. She didn't know what to do.

On the plus side, she would advance from being an intern to being officially on staff, which meant she would have an actual paycheck, albeit a small one. On the minus side, she would be essentially on her own (despite the title of acting state field director, her entire paid staff would consist of one: herself), setting up a statewide operation with little money in her pocket, a young black woman in the Deep South in a city where she knew no one. Wouldn't she be way out of her depth? she wondered.

"Sava," I said, "I think this will be a really great experience for you. You're going to learn so much." And it was that last point that convinced her to take the position.

Here is how Sava remembers that conversation:

"You didn't say, 'Oh, everything's going to be great, Sava, you'll do just fine.' You told me it would be hard. But I knew I could talk to you if I felt afraid. And you helped me see that I would be making a contribution not only to the campaign but also to myself and my own professional abilities. I just had to trust that it would be okay."

Sava says it was one of the scariest decisions she has ever made, but she was able to do it because she had someone supporting her: she had me as a mentor.

She moved to Alabama, and with her tiny state field director's pay managed to find a way to live. She opened four offices throughout Alabama, organized volunteers, and (eventually) hired additional staff in preparation for Alabama's primary on Super Tuesday, which also happened to be the day of nearly two dozen other state primaries. Obama won Alabama with a decisive

56 percent of the vote and twenty-seven of the state's fifty-two delegates.

"I learned a lot about what I was capable of, and about myself as a person," says Sava. "The experience gave me a broader perspective on how I can make a contribution to society. It was difficult, but I would do it all again."

She adds, "You have a job for a season, and an experience for a moment, but your relationships are forever. I feel so blessed to be surrounded in my life by people who believe in me. I can get through any hurdle or difficult time, because of the support I have."

After the campaign Sava was accepted into Yale Law School, where she is pursuing a law degree with plans to eventually pursue an MBA from Harvard.

The benefits of mentorship go both ways. Sava continues to be a big part of my life, and I gain as much from our relationship as she does. Knowing her gives me a valuable perspective that comes from her wisdom, which goes far beyond her years.

Often we don't fully realize what we know until we hear ourselves sharing it with others. You're never too old to learn—or too knowledgeable.

TAKE THE INITIATIVE TO SEEK OUT MENTORS

Sometimes the people we work with, such as a direct supervisor or team leader, serve as strong mentors to us. At other times, we may be fortunate to have mentors unexpectedly appear in our lives, as happened with me and Elliott Masie. Often, though, it is up to us to actively seek them out.

"Who are your most important mentors?" When I ask this question, people typically talk about their parents or grandparents, or a teacher or coach they had in school. Yet I am often surprised that the answers all seem to be about mentors in the distant past. The need for strong mentors doesn't stop when we become adults; it continues throughout our lives.

Every time I begin a new job, join a new organization, or enter a new field, I seek out new mentors who can show me the ropes. Amy Millman did this for me when I was new in Washington. She had been a lobbyist there for years when I arrived, and her wisdom, insights, and candor saved me a good deal of trial and error. She also became my good friend and greatest collaborator.

A mentor isn't necessarily someone who is a lot older than you are, but is someone who has a different expertise or experience. My sister Dee Dee is a year younger than I am, but she has always been a source of great wisdom and perspective for me. She was especially helpful to me in my White House role, having been there herself for two years before me. In some ways my daughter, Madison, is a mentor to me; her fresh perspective on the world has given me new ways to think about things—as well as a better command of the remote control and computer.

I think one reason we don't actively seek out mentors more often is that we sometimes let our own insecurity hold us back. It may be that we feel vulnerable asking for help, or believe that it's too much to ask, that "they're probably too busy." But the truth is, people are almost always flattered to be asked for their help.

At a recent Kennedy School reunion, a young woman named Victoria Salinas approached me and asked if I would be willing to spend a little time with her on the phone for some career advice. I told her I'd be happy to, and we scheduled a time to speak.

As we talked, I learned that she had joined FEMA after Hurricane Katrina as a Presidential Management Fellow and was now a deputy branch chief. Having worked internationally in postconflict countries, she was moved to help her own country rebuild. Through the fellowship program, she had been able to pursue many professional development opportunities and take on prominent leadership roles, which had afforded her the opportunity to exercise her innate leadership abilities—but she lacked inspiring role models in her day-to-day life.

"I love working in this field," she said, "but I would really like to have a mentor. I would love to get your advice on how to go about doing that."

"Is there anyone there at FEMA whom you admire or feel you could learn from?" I asked.

Yes, she said, and she told me about Bill Carwile. Now associate administrator of Response and Recovery and one of the top people at FEMA, Carwile had served the nation abroad and at home, in war, and after catastrophic disasters. His core value, said Victoria, seemed to be that "people matter," and he was admired and respected by everyone who worked with him. "He is the kind of leader I want to be one day."

"Why don't you ask him if he would be your mentor?" I suggested.

She was concerned that he was too high in the chain of command and would be too busy. I encouraged her to ask anyway. "What do you have to lose? He can always say no. Maybe send him or his assistant a quick email, ask for a few minutes on his schedule and say you have a question to ask him."

She emailed me later to tell me that she'd done exactly what we discussed; in fact, she did it that same day.

"I shot off an email with the subject line 'Non-Work Related Question.' It said, 'Dear Mr. Carwile, Can we meet? I have something I'd like to ask you.' Not even an hour had passed when I got an email instructing me to schedule time with his administrative assistant."

They met, and she shared her predicament, her respect for him as a leader, and that she felt she could learn tremendously from him. Then she asked him if he would be open to mentoring her.

"His response could not have been more positive. He readily said yes, was touched that I'd asked him, and wanted to know specifically what my vision was for a mentor-mentee relationship so we could use our time together constructively."

Later he sent her an email thanking her for having the confidence in him to serve as her mentor. He added:

"My views: leadership is not an inherent skill. It, like many other skills, requires nurturing and development. I have learned this from personal experience over decades of leading and following."

In that initial meeting, he gave her a homework assignment, asking her to define the qualities of a leader and rating herself on those attributes. He sent her to a leadership training in Texas, and when she came back, asked her to write up an action plan for how she could go about implementing what she had learned there. Since that time they have continued meeting every three weeks.

"Just as he is mentoring me," she adds, "I am now having the opportunity to coach and mentor some of the new Presidential Management Fellows at FEMA. The joy of helping them out along the way is tremendous."

She is thrilled at how it has worked out—and all she needed to do was ask.

LEARNING FROM VALLEYS

There is one more source of learning I want to mention, one that can be even more powerful than the best adviser or mentor, that greatest teacher of all: adversity.

On the evening of January 7, 2008, I was part of a gathering of Obama supporters at the home of Gary and Meg Hirshberg. The successful cofounder of Stonyfield Farm yogurt company, Gary was an early Obama supporter in New Hampshire, and he and Meg were on the advisory board for the New Hampshire campaign. Gathered in their beautiful home that evening were other members of the advisory board, along with National Finance Committee members and a variety of elected officials from around the country who had all flown in to help with the get-out-the-vote effort.

There was no doubt in this house that we would win the New Hampshire primary the following day, and by a sizable margin at that. Only five short days ago, to the surprise of much of the country, we had won the Iowa caucuses by nine points. The national polls were predicting an Obama win here by *seventeen* points.

I asked Joel Bennenson, one of our campaign pollsters, if he agreed that we would win by that sizable a margin. "Is it really seventeen points, Joel?" I asked.

"Oh, we won't win by seventeen," he replied. "Our internal polling shows closer to ten."

On the New Hampshire staff call with Senator Obama that night, even the usually cautious candidate sounded a confident note. It looked like we had this one sewn up.

But we did not.

When we woke up to an uncharacteristically warm New Hampshire morning on January 8, the day brought a very different outcome. We did not win by seventeen points, nor by ten points. In fact, we *lost* the New Hampshire primary to Hillary Clinton by a two-point margin.

To the staff, volunteers, and advisory board, many of whom had given a year of their lives to the cause, the news was devastating.

Like the rest of us, Senator Obama was both surprised and disappointed by the loss. But instead of acting upset, he responded to this huge setback with reflection and resolve: "Okay, what can we learn from this?" As he said in his remarks the next day at an event in Boston, "We were like Icarus, flying too close to the sun."

The silver lining of our New Hampshire defeat was that we *did* learn from it, and we were able to move on to the rest of the campaign with the added benefit of this shared experience. It was a reminder that every single voter in every single state mattered, and that we needed to treat each state as if it were our final and most decisive contest. Rather than feeling beaten down by the loss, we were able to use this defeat to move forward with new resolve, fresh insights, and greater awareness.

In retrospect, I believe this unexpected loss was the best thing that happened to the Obama campaign. Had we won New Hampshire, the outcome of the entire presidential primary contest may have been quite different. The event galvanized the teams on the ground, and the campaign became committed to never take anything for granted again.

What is especially interesting to note is that we did in fact find ourselves facing a similar situation toward the end of the general campaign eight months later, when the polls were predicting a double-digit lead over John McCain. This time, though, we had learned from New Hampshire—and rather than slip into complacency, we redoubled our efforts as if we were coming from a distant second place. As Senator Obama put it, "We don't want to wake up on the morning of November 5 and ask ourselves, Was there one more thing we could have done?"

A few months after the election, my friend and mentor Spencer Johnson published another of his wonderful parables, *Peaks and Valleys*. In that book Spencer writes:

Peaks And Valleys are connected.

The Errors You Make In
Today's Good Times
Create Tomorrow's Bad Times.

And The Wise Things You Do In
Today's Bad Times
Create Tomorrow's Good Times.

Our defeat in New Hampshire was one of the deepest valleys of the campaign, but it was how we dealt with that valley that led to the peaks of the Democratic nomination and, ultimately, the election.

It is often in times of defeat that we see a leader's true core. It is easy to be calm and confident when you are winning, but it is times of difficulty and disappointment that offer the greatest opportunities for learning and growth.

How to Take the Lead

It's easy to become complacent, to reach certain levels in our career where our learning becomes stagnant. But the world never stands still, and there are always new things to learn. Leaders never stop challenging and pushing themselves to learn more.

- Do you regularly take on new and different challenges, and put yourself in a position where you have to learn?

- In whatever area you work, do you thoroughly know your material? Effective leaders are always pushing the envelope of their knowledge and mastery of their area.

- Do you regularly step outside of your own experience, sit down, and talk with people in your organization? One way leaders learn is to get outside the bubble of their own experience or comfort zone and discover what is happening in the lives of people around them.

- Are you creating an atmosphere in your organization where your people are willing to tell you the truth? Most of the answers you need are usually right there within your own team, provided you are willing to listen—and they feel safe enough to tell you.

- Do you have your own personal advisory board? If not, you can create one. Surround yourself with people who will give you support, expertise, and critical perspective you wouldn't have on your own.

- Who are your mentors? A mentor brings out your most productive feelings and qualities by the way he or she supports, nurtures, guides, and acknowledges you. Mentors see things in you that you don't see in yourself.

- Do you actively seek out mentors? Every time you begin a new job, join a new organization, or enter a new field, it makes sense to seek out new mentors who can show you the ropes. Find those in your field whom you respect, admire, and feel you could learn from, and ask if they have the time to mentor you. Most people will be flattered you asked.

- How do you view setbacks and failures? Usually such difficult times offer the greatest opportunities to learn valuable lessons that can give you the critical edge in future situations. As Spencer Johnson says, "The errors you make in today's good times create tomorrow's bad times—and the wise things you do in today's bad times create tomorrow's good times."

7. COURAGE

Bright Lights in Dark Days

Authenticity, the desire to connect, respect, clarity, the willingness to collaborate, and a lifelong appetite for learning . . . these are all critical ingredients, but I believe it takes one additional character trait to bring all these together. This last trait has been clearly present, hovering in the background in many of the stories I've shared even though we haven't singled it out. I wanted to save it for last. This trait is *courage*.

I believe that fear is the number one obstacle that holds us back from doing what we truly want in life. Leaders are not necessarily fearless, but they are people who have learned how to confront and push through their fears.

Courage is about pushing through our fears to live our most authentic life and do what we believe is right. Fear turns opportunity into obstacles. It takes courage to live our convictions, to persevere, to take risks, to tell the truth, to apologize and admit mistakes. It takes courage to live consciously, seeking the truth that may be causing pain to ourselves, the people we love, or those we work with. Another of my favorite Eleanor Roosevelt quotes sums it up perfectly:

"We gain strength, and courage, and confidence by each experience in which we really stop to look fear in the face . . . we must do that which we think we cannot."

It's one thing to say, "Push through your fear," but how do we actually do it? One powerful first step is to identify the source of your fear, that is, to pin down exactly what it is you're really afraid of.

As a simple example, one of the most common fears is the fear of public speaking. (Some surveys have found that for many, this fear ranks even above the fear of dying!) But is it really fear of speaking itself, or is it perhaps the fear of standing up there in front of all those people and suddenly not remembering what you were going to say?

Toastmasters International has helped tens of thousands of people overcome their fear of public speaking by showing them how to prepare their material. Once you really know your material, how you're going to begin and how you're going to end, your confidence grows and becomes stronger than the fear. It doesn't mean you don't still have a few butterflies in your stomach, but they don't stop you. When you feel prepared, it allows you to summon the courage to get up on the stage.

"YOU HAVE TO GO ON TO THE NEXT GRADE"

I saw a very poignant example of this with my daughter, Madison, a few years ago.

In January 2008, Madison entered a two-year program that included both kindergarteners and first-graders, so that she would be spending the next eighteen months in the same class. We had just moved back to Boston from Chicago, where Madison had spent the first semester of kindergarten, and it was in some ways a difficult transition for her.

Madison adored her new teacher, Kathleen Fucci. Kathleen's steady and loving nature was an important influence during this time, and I will be forever grateful to her for the nurturing role she played in Madison's life.

That spring, I was making lunch for my daughter one morning as we were getting ready for school, when I discovered we were out of bread for sandwiches.

"Madison," I said, "we're out of bread. Hot lunch today, okay?"

To my surprise, she became very upset and starting crying, almost to the point of hysteria. I was taken aback by her strong reaction. I stopped what I was doing and went over to her. "Madison," I said, "have you ever had hot lunch at your new school before?"

With tears streaming down her face, she shook her head. *No.*

"Are you feeling afraid?"

She nodded her head. *Yes.*

We proceeded on to school and I walked my still crying daughter to her classroom with her tiny hand clasped in mine. I reassured her that I would not leave until we understood what needed to be done to get her hot lunch and she felt safe.

When we entered her classroom, Mrs. Fucci met us at the door. She could see that Madison was upset. I explained the situation. She understood immediately and took Madison's hand.

"Come with me," she said, and they walked together over to a table where Mrs. Fucci picked up a small white bucket, which she showed to Madison. "When you are having hot lunch," she explained, "you take the clothespin—the one with your name on it—and attach it to the bucket. That is how we let the kitchen know how many lunches to expect."

Then she assigned Madison a buddy, a classmate named Rachael, to show her the ropes that first day. Rachael, she explained, would walk with Madison at lunchtime, show her what to do, and sit with her.

Madison stopped crying immediately. I left my little girl that day knowing she was in good hands.

That evening, I asked her how it went getting hot lunch. "Great!" she said. "In fact, I want to get hot lunch again tomorrow."

"That's great, Madison!"

She looked up at me with her serious eyes and said, "Mommy, I pushed through my fear today."

Rachael became Madison's best friend (she was the girl who inspired Madison to start dancing), and the following autumn, Madison in turn played the role of lunch buddy to new kindergarten students.

Whether we are five or eighty-five, we all have new situations arise that challenge our comfort level. It is when we *push through our fear* to stretch and grow that we gain confidence.

One day the following spring, as she neared the end of her two years with Mrs. Fucci, Madison told me that she loved her teacher so much, it would be okay with her if she repeated first grade. I completely understood her attachment to her wonderful teacher, and wondered how things would go for Madison when the time actually came to say good-bye to Mrs. Fucci's classroom.

Finally the day came: the very last day of first grade. I picked Madison up from school, and as we walked home I asked her how it felt to be finished with first grade—and if she felt sad to say good-bye to Mrs. Fucci.

"Mommy, I was brave." She thought about it for a moment more, then turned to me and said, "You have to go on to the next grade."

School years document the natural progression and growth of our childhoods, but we should never stop reaching for the next level in our lives. Having the courage and curiosity to *go on to the next grade*—to move into unfamiliar territory and try new adventures—is what allows us to stretch and grow. It keeps us interested in life and interesting to be around.

A LIGHT IN DARK DAYS

Sometimes the greatest act of courage is to follow your heart and do the right thing, even if it isn't popular—or, in some cases, even if it doesn't seem politically expedient. One of my favorite moments of witnessing this kind of courage occurred during the early months of the Obama campaign, when the nomination was still a long way off and seemed a next-to-impossible goal.

The summer of 2007 brought some dark days for the Obama campaign. By July, we were trailing in the national polls by thirty points. The negative press about the campaign and candidate's standing was at a high point. While we focused doggedly on our early-states strategy, we also dealt with input from increasingly frustrated supporters across the country who were losing faith and calling for changes in our strategy.

Morale was especially low at the Chicago headquarters. This was partly due to the news coverage and polls throughout the summer. For example (one of many), the Zogby International poll showed Hillary Clinton moving past John Edwards to take the lead in Iowa, with Clinton leading by 30 percent, followed by Edwards at 23 percent and Obama at 10 percent, with the rest of the contenders taking 3 percent or less.

Another factor in the low morale was that the Chicago team did not have the constant boosts of inspiration that those in the field experienced. Unlike the teams in the early states, who saw the candidate, heard the speeches, experienced the crowds, witnessed the turnouts, and helped build the relationships in the field, the Chicago staff was insulated from the excitement on the ground.

But then, on July 26, the campaign got an unexpected boost: Paul Hodes, the freshman congressman from New Hampshire, called a press conference and told the world that he had decided to endorse Barack Obama's candidacy for president.

As the news went out to the campaign staff via email, you could hear people hooting and shouting throughout headquarters. Paul's vote of confidence gave everyone an unexpected shot in the arm that came exactly when it was most needed. "Hodes has endorsed!" It was an extraordinary act of courage that was both personally meaningful and strategically significant.

THE AUDACITY OF HODES

It was not lost on any of us that this was not only a bold move for Congressman Hodes but also a politically risky one. Paul had come from behind to win his seat the previous November and now held the prestigious position of president of the 2006 Democratic freshman class. He had been in office barely six months, and staking his political fortunes on Barack Obama's unlikely candidacy, at a time when Hillary Clinton's nomination was widely seen as a foregone conclusion, was an extraordinary gamble. The New Hampshire primary was still a very long six months away. The politically smart thing to do would probably have been to wait at least a few more months, if not longer, and see how the race was shaping up.

Instead, Paul decided to trust his instinct, even if it meant risking his political future. He went to his staff and told them he had decided to endorse Senator Obama. Not surprisingly, they responded with caution. "It's awfully early to endorse," they told him.

"Early's important," he replied. "Early counts more than later. My heart tells me this, my mind tells me this, and I don't care about the polling."

He called a press conference in downtown Concord, his hometown, and told reporters he was officially endorsing the freshman senator from Chicago.

"Barack and I share an optimistic vision for this country," he told the several hundred supporters packed into Concord's Eagle Square, "and we share the belief that change is possible when people come together."

Reaction came swiftly.

"My colleagues in Congress thought I'd lost my marbles," recalls Paul. "I got a lot of ribbing in the clerk room and on the floor. 'You're a freshman congressman. What have you done?!'"

He also got quite a bit of negative reaction from many among his constituents. At the same time, he says, it also turned some heads and made people think.

"A lot of people told me that my endorsement, unlike other endorsements, actually meant a lot to them," Paul later told me. "It caused them to really examine their views, to take a couple of steps back and look again."

And it didn't end with his endorsement. Once Paul made his decision, that was that. "My father taught me, once you've made your decision you just go with it," says Paul. "What's the point of looking back?"

The trend of negative press continued well past the summer months. In late September, even after a rally for Senator Obama drew a crowd of 24,000 in New York City and the campaign had raised $20 million in the third quarter (with an estimated $80 million for the year, putting the Obama campaign on a par with the Clinton campaign), the front-page headline of *USA Today* blared, BARACK OBAMA CAN'T GET TRACTION. In October, when the polls were still down, Paul went to the national finance committee and said, "Pay no attention to the polls. Barack is going to be the next president. Have no doubt, have no fear, and let's go."

Keith Johnstone, the British father of improvisational theater, says in his classic 1979 text *Impro: Improvisation and the Theatre:*

> There are people who prefer to say "Yes," and there are people who prefer to say "No." Those who say "Yes" are rewarded by the adventures they have, and those who say "No" are rewarded by the safety they attain. There are far more "No" sayers around than "Yes" sayers.

Paul Hodes had the guts to be one of the early "Yes" sayers.

I first met Congressman Hodes and his wife, Peggo, at the big Oprah rally for Senator Obama in Manchester, New Hampshire, on December 8. That night I shared with Paul what his early endorsement had meant to the campaign. His gesture of courage and personal leadership was one of those moments that really mattered.

I asked him what made him make that early decision.

"During the summer Peggo and I talked about it and what it would mean," he replied. "I know a lot of people thought of it as courageous. To me, it was simply the right thing to do. If there was some small thing I could do to change the course of our country and help make it the kind of place we know it can be, then I couldn't live with myself if I *didn't* do it."

Paul was not alone for long. That evening his fellow New Hampshire representative, Carol Shea-Porter, also endorsed Obama. With the first primary still a month away, this, too, was a courageous move. But Paul's public statement of endorsement came first, and I will always think of it as *the audacity of Hodes*.

THE COURAGE TO DEMAND EXCELLENCE

A wonderful example of courage under fire is my friend Deborah Gist, Rhode Island's commissioner of education. I knew Deb from the Kennedy School, where we were classmates in the MPA program; we both graduated in 2000. Ten years later, in May 2010, she was named one of *Time* magazine's "world's 100 most influential people," an honor she earned in part for her courageous stand in her commitment to bring a better quality of education to the children of Rhode Island.

In the summer of 2009, when Deb assumed her position in Rhode Island, the state's school system was ranked among the poorest-performing in the nation in its education of black and Hispanic students, a situation Deb was determined to change.

She started by visiting every one of the state's thirty-six school districts, meeting with students, faculty, and administrators to learn as much as she could about what was working, what wasn't, and what changes were needed, and to identify the lowest-performing schools. In these meetings, she repeatedly shared her commitment to make decisions based on what was best for the students.

"You can say that in a roomful of people," says Deb, "and everyone nods and agrees—but when you actually start to implement that, and it means that adults are going to have to change their behaviors, practices, or habits, then it's a whole different conversation."

Deb soon began creating sweeping changes. She announced that staffing decisions would now be based on teacher qualifications rather than on seniority, and put in place a new evaluation system based on annual reviews (an idea practiced in only fifteen other states). "When she learned that Rhode Island's teacher-training programs had one of the lowest test-score requirements for entrance," as the *Time* story reported, "she found out which state set the bar the highest—then raised Rhode Island's one point above that." [1]

One of the schools identified as most needing attention was Central Falls High School, which had a 50 percent dropout rate and fewer than one in ten students able to do math at their grade level. Deb tasked that district's superintendent, Frances Gallo, with the necessary guidelines to work with the district stakeholders—from administrators and faculty to teachers' union and community members—to come up with a change model. After coming to initial agreement with the stakeholders, they ran into difficulty: a combination of conflicting interests and resistance from the teachers' union slowed the process to a crawl.

Eventually, frustrated with the lack of forward motion, Superintendent Gallo recommended a more radical model that involved letting go of all the school's faculty, with the intention of hiring back the top-performing 50 percent. (Because of a deadline set forth in state law, the time frame required the termination of *all* teachers, which would have been followed by the rehiring of up to 50 percent.) Deb approved and supported the plan.

The situation soon drew national attention and earned her

---

1. Amanda Ripley, "Deborah Gist—The 2010 Time 100," *Time*, April 29, 2010.
    From *Time*'s "The World's Most Influential People."

COURAGE   201

widespread support and accolades, including endorsement from
US secretary of education Arne Duncan and President Obama. At
the same time, Deb has taken a lot of heat, too, and the situation
has been a painful one.

"I try to explain to our critics that we were not blaming the
teachers for the school's underperformance," says Deb. "I have
tremendous respect for teachers. I started out as an elementary
school teacher. I wanted to engage them and gain their commitment to being part of the change. But some people latch on to a
part of the story they feel is unjust and draw conclusions about our
motives and intentions."

Deb says she acted out of her love for and commitment to the
students.

"You have to know what is your North Star, what is the thing
that is driving you when you make the hard decisions. For me, the
students are always in the forefront.

"Sometimes you have to make decisions not everyone is going
to be comfortable with. You have to focus on what you are trying
to accomplish, with as much respect and care as you can for everyone involved. But you can't let that stop you from what needs to
be done. At the same time, you can't alienate everyone. Leadership
takes courage—but courage without being reckless."

Deb points out that really difficult issues like this rarely have
easy or clear-cut solutions.

"The safer thing is not to take the risk at all—and that is where
courage comes in. Courage is the willingness to make the decision,
based on the information you have, and knowing that you could be
wrong. Courage is being willing to take that risk."

In the end, they were able to come back together with the union
and arrive at an even better solution that involved hiring back all

the original teachers and building upon the original model that Deb and Dr. Gallo had first proposed.

"You always want to go back to trying to build a relationship," says Deb. "You can never close a door and say, because of that conflict we will never be able to work together again. If that happens, you are on the road to failure. You always have to be willing to come back together and say, What did we learn from this and how do we move forward?"

THE UNPOPULAR TRUTH

Sometimes courage is a matter of speaking up and giving voice to an uncomfortable truth.

In early March 2008, the Obama campaign faced a painful and difficult conflict when WABC-TV aired some particularly controversial clips from the sermons of Obama's longtime pastor, Reverend Jeremiah Wright, at the Trinity United Church of Christ in Chicago.

A month earlier, Barack Obama and Hillary Clinton had seen a virtual tie in the Super Tuesday primaries, and the flurry of primaries in the weeks since had basically followed the same trend. Now there was a lull, with no primaries for a full seven weeks while everyone prepared for the crucial Pennsylvania contest. With the two leading Democratic contenders neck and neck and no new primaries to report on, the media was hungry for anything that could spice up the news cycle and give the race traction in either direction. Archive footage of Reverend Wright's more pungent sermons was just what the doctor ordered.

Reverend Wright had been a fierce critic of American foreign and domestic policy, and was especially vehement in his denunciation of white racism and the treatment of blacks in America. "The government . . . wants us to sing God *bless* America?" went a clip from a 2003 rant. "No, no, God *damn* America!"

Now Senator Obama was being accused of being close friends with a radical pastor whose political views were at odds with what the candidate himself had been saying on the campaign trail. There was a growing anxiety about this issue across the country from the press, supporters, and voters. The Reverend Wright issue was starting to spiral out of control and threatened to derail the campaign.

On March 18, addressing a crowd in Philadelphia's National Constitution Center just steps away from Independence Hall, candidate Obama addressed the Reverend Wright issue head-on, in a speech titled "A More Perfect Union" that spoke directly to the issue of race in America. This was not a campaign strategy or public-relations maneuver; it was his idea to give the speech and the words came from his authentic self. He stayed up into the early-morning hours during the two days beforehand writing it.

Pundits later said it was one of the greatest speeches in American history. To me, it was one of his most courageous acts of the campaign.

The politically expedient option might have been to throw Reverend Wright under the bus, but this he would not do, no matter how awkward or hateful the pastor's widely circulating statements. He did not defend Jeremiah Wright's remarks, but he also did not rush to distance himself.

There were those supporters who fervently hoped that he would disown Wright. Instead, he chose to talk about his relationship to the pastor in the context of the painful and difficult issue of race in America.

I can no more disown him than I can disown the black community. I can no more disown him than I can my white grandmother—a woman who helped raise me, a woman who sacrificed again and again for me, a woman who loves me as much as she loves anything in this world, but a woman who once confessed her fear of black men who passed by her on the street, and who on more than one occasion has uttered racial or ethnic stereotypes that made me cringe.

These people are a part of me. And they are a part of America, this country that I love.

Some will see this as an attempt to justify or excuse comments that are simply inexcusable. I can assure you it is not. I suppose the politically safe thing would be to move on from this episode and just hope it fades into the woodwork. We can dismiss Reverend Wright as a crank or a demagogue, just as we have dismissed Geraldine Ferraro, in the aftermath of her recent statements, as harboring some deep-seated racial bias.

But race is an issue that I believe this nation cannot afford to ignore right now. We would be making the same mistake that Reverend Wright made in his offending sermons about America—to simplify and stereotype and amplify the negative to the point that it distorts reality.

The fact is that the comments that have been made and the issues that have surfaced over the last few weeks reflect the complexities of race in this country that we've never really worked through—a part of our union that we have yet to perfect. And if we walk away now, if we simply retreat into our respective corners, we will never be able to come together to solve challenges like health care, or education, or the need to find good jobs for every American.

That is where we are right now. It's a racial stalemate we've been stuck in for years. Contrary to the claims of some of my critics, black and white, I have never been so naïve as to believe that we can get beyond our racial divisions in a single election cycle, or with a single candidacy—particularly a candidacy as imperfect as my own. But I have asserted a firm conviction—a conviction rooted in my faith in God and my faith in the American people—that working together we can move beyond some of our old racial wounds, and that in fact we have no choice if we are to continue on the path of a more perfect union.

That speech was a turning point. It got the campaign back on track, and I could feel its impact as I traveled around the country.

A month later, a woman at a town hall meeting in Kentucky where I was speaking stood up and said, "When Barack put his name in the ring, I sent you five dollars, because that's what I could afford to send. And when he gave his speech on race and had the courage to talk the truth to such an important, unspoken issue in our country, I sent you another five dollars."

Of all the moments when I felt proud to be a part of this historic effort, this one made me especially proud.

Throughout history we have most admired those leaders who demonstrate the courage to speak the truth, even when the truth was unpopular; to operate from conviction, even when expediency would reveal an easier path; to face an unpopular issue, champion an important cause, and stand tall in times of trial.

ELECTION DAY

Sometimes "doing the right thing" means doing the right thing for *you* and your family. These are often tough decisions, and they may be private decisions that nobody but you ever witnesses—but they can be among the most important decisions in your life.

On November 4, 2008, I was all set to leave for an overnight trip to Chicago. It was Election Day, the culmination of two long years of incredibly hard work and a critical moment in the history of our nation. I had planned to be in Chicago's Grant Park to share election night with fellow campaign staff and supporters. It would also be an opportunity to reconnect and celebrate with supporters and teammates who had become my friends. But when I woke up that morning, it suddenly hit me: "What am I doing?!"

The two years I had spent on the campaign would not have been possible if it had not been for the constancy and support of my family. They *were* my teammates, and there was nowhere else I would rather be than home, sharing this historic moment with the people I loved most.

I canceled my trip to Chicago.

Like everyone else in the country (and many around the world), we stayed up late into the night with a mixture of antici-pation, relief, disbelief, and excitement. We had come so far over the twenty-two months since my first meeting in Senator Obama's Senate office that January 2007 day. As exciting as it was, it was also bittersweet for me, as the night marked the end to this chapter of my life.

The next morning I took Madison to school. About to walk into the school building, she stopped, turned around, and asked me to kneel down so she could see my face. I could see that she had something she wanted to tell me.

During the general election, Madison had actually declared herself in favor of McCain. On Election Day, as she drove with Rob and me to the polls, she kept reminding Rob that he was supposed to vote for John McCain. Now, standing with me at the entrance to her school, she hugged me and kissed my cheeks, and then she said, "Mommy, you know I really always wanted Barack to win. I just didn't want him to take you away anymore."

During my two years on the campaign trail, I saw people give of themselves—give their time, their money, give up their jobs, their security, give virtually everything they had in pursuit of this dream that they believed in so strongly. My daughter's sacrifice included—although this was *not* her choice. When I had shared my worries with other mothers in the campaign about how hard this was on Madison, they were always very supportive. "It may seem hard now," they would say, "but when your daughter grows up, she will be so proud of you. She'll know and understand that her sacrifice was worth it," they would assure me. "She'll be able to tell her friends that her own mother played a big role in the election of the country's first African-American president."

"She's only five, Betsy," one fellow supporter added. "She won't even remember your not being there."

I would tell myself that they were right, that what I was doing was very important, was history-making, was the chance of a lifetime, and that it would all be worth it. But I knew in my heart of hearts that this was not entirely true, that it would never totally compensate for all the days I lost being with my little girl.

For two years, my family had been on the back burner, and I knew it was time now to shift my priorities. The obvious next step would have been to pursue a position in the Obama administration—but I decided against this path. This would mean my next career move would be taking a step out into the unknown. With no clear job or position in front of me, moving forward would mean making a conscious choice to step into ambiguity.

Sometimes that is the definition of courage: being willing to *step into ambiguity* and take a new path, even when you don't have any idea what that path will look like. Giving yourself the time to explore and not have it all figured out. Often, once you summon the courage to take this step, it turns out to open up wonderful new possibilities that otherwise might have remained closed or hidden.

That night, I received an email out of the blue, inviting me to give a talk on leadership. Unexpected as it was, this turned out to be the beginning of a whole new direction for me. I didn't know it yet, but my leap of faith had already sown the seeds of a new career.

Madison was right. Sometimes you just have to let go and go on to the next grade.

How to Take the Lead

Leaders are not necessarily fearless, but they have learned how to deal with their fears. It takes courage to live our convictions, persevere, take risks, tell the truth, apologize, and admit mistakes. Courage is about pushing through our fears to live our most authentic life and do what we believe is right.

- Does your current work feel fresh, challenging, and engaging? Having the courage to *go on to the next grade,* to move into unfamiliar territory and try new adventures, is what allows us to stretch and grow.

- Sometimes the greatest act of courage is to follow your heart and do the right thing, even if it isn't popular or doesn't seem politically expedient. What is your North Star, that thing that most drives you when you have to make the hard decisions?

- Are you willing to speak up and give voice to an uncomfortable truth or unpopular issue?

- Are you willing to risk being wrong? Sometimes leadership takes having the courage to make hard decisions based on the best information you have, knowing that you could be wrong. At the same time, you can't alienate everyone. Leadership takes courage—but courage without being reckless.

- Do you give yourself credit for those tough decisions that nobody else sees? Sometimes doing the right thing means making private decisions that no one but you ever witnesses—but they can be among the most important decisions in your life.

- Do you give yourself the permission to make hard decisions without necessarily having it all figured out? Are you willing to *step into ambiguity* when the occasion calls for it? Once you summon the courage to take this step, it often opens up wonderful new possibilities that otherwise might have remained closed or hidden.

CONCLUSION

Being Conscious

This book has sought to bring awareness to a simple belief about leadership: when leaders are committed to bringing out their people's most productive feelings, it makes for happier people *and* more productive work environments. Throughout my career, I have observed this in others and seen it in myself. I've seen my own productivity and success magnified in situations where I felt appreciated and valued—and have felt my energy and enthusiasm flag in those circumstances where that wasn't the case. You probably know what that difference feels like, too. I think everyone does.

If I were to recommend a single leadership skill to any organization, public or private, large or small, it would be this: put your focus on whether your leaders and managers are bringing out the most productive feelings of their people. How do you know? You'll know because when they are, you'll see an organization full of people who feel a deep sense of connection and commitment to the organization and its mission, who are willing to take the lead and go the extra mile.

What does that look like? It looks something like a scene that unfolded one day, not long ago, at the ticket counter of a major airline.

A young woman approached the ticket counter and hurriedly

explained to the agent on duty that she didn't have a ticket, but was desperate to get on the next flight, which was headed for the city where her husband was stationed. "He is about to deploy to Afghanistan," she explained. "If I don't board this flight, I won't be able to meet up with him before he leaves."

The agent, Nancy Villarreal, consulted a colleague, Reenie Prine, and together they quickly found the woman the lowest fare available for the departing flight: $179 one-way. The woman burst into tears. She had only $79, she explained between sobs. A hundred dollars short, she wouldn't be able to make the flight. And that would have been that, if this had been any typical airline—but it wasn't: it was Southwest Airlines, and what happened next speaks volumes about the company's culture and leadership.

A third agent, Anita Christerson, came over to see what the commotion was about. When she heard the story, she whipped out her credit card and insisted on paying for the woman's flight, urging her to keep the $79 she had on hand for her travel expenses. Nancy and Reenie immediately joined the cause and pulled out their own credit cards, splitting the woman's ticket three ways. The grateful young woman boarded the flight and was able to meet up with her husband and say good-bye in person before he deployed overseas.[1]

To me, what makes this story so amazing is that *it is not that unusual*—at least not in the culture of Southwest Airlines. At Southwest, such spontaneous acts of human kindness and personal caring happen all the time. Why? What's their secret? It comes down to having a culture of *engagement*.

---

1. This story appeared in the June 2010 edition of *LUVLines*, the monthly newsletter for Southwest Airlines employees.

In July 2010, I visited Southwest headquarters in Dallas to speak at their Leadership Summit, which brought together 700 of their senior managers from across the country. While I was there I learned about an employee engagement survey that had just been conducted by Mercer, the prestigious HR consulting firm. Among other results, the study found that 92 percent of Southwest's employees felt they had a personal impact on the company's bottom line; the level of employee commitment was also 92 percent; and the number of employees who agreed with the statement "I can meet my career goals at Southwest" was again 92 percent.

And the number of employees who described themselves as "Willing to go the extra mile for the company"? This one was not 92 percent—it was 97 percent.

I asked Elizabeth Bryant, Southwest's director of talent development, what she felt created such extraordinary results. She replied: "As a company, we put our employees at the center of our decision making. Taking care of our employees is a priority. When you do that, you have employees who are committed to the cause, who recognize that this is a career, and not just a job.

"Other companies ask us, 'How do you create this kind of culture and success?' My response is, *We care about our people*. We want to serve each other and be authentic about who we are. Everything else just falls into place."

Walking through Southwest's headquarters, I noticed that the walls were lined with pictures of employees, each wall dedicated to a different theme: one was reserved for wedding photos, another for employees' children, another for pets, and another for sports. It felt so personal, as if I were walking through someone's home. (I learned that there is one staff member whose full-time job is to collect, frame, and hang these photos!)

Over the years I have experienced a great many workplaces, but
it is rare to find a work environment that features so many happy
people and such a palpable sense of camaraderie. Everywhere I
went, employees shared one story after another that showed how
connected, supported, and engaged they felt in this community.
Several people told me how important it was to them that company
cofounder Herb Kelleher and president emerita Colleen Barrett
knew all their names and remembered important events in their
lives—and they pointed out that Gary Kelly, the current CEO,
shared that same ability and personal touch.

"We are a family," says Colleen Barrett. "We celebrate together
and we grieve together. If our employees are hurt, we hurt with
them. I'm not saying it's all wine and roses every day. But people
here enjoy what they do and genuinely care about each other. It's
intangible and hard to measure, but it's very real." [2]

And *that* is what lay behind those three ticket agents' spontaneous decision to pay for that young woman's airline ticket out
of their own pockets. It was a natural gesture that flowed directly
from the people-focused culture at Southwest.

This is not simply a matter of "soft" values, of creating an atmosphere of warm fuzzy feelings purely for its own sake. It's nice to
be nice—but the bottom line is that this approach is also *profitable*.
Over the past decade, throughout the post-9/11 downturn, the following years of soaring energy costs, and the recent catastrophic
global recession, Southwest has survived and thrived—with no
layoffs. They have kept costs well below the industry average, all
while maintaining revenues that have consistently outperformed

---

2. John David Mann, "A Company in Love," *Networking Times*, January/February
2010.

those of their competitors. During that same time they have become the number one airline in the world as measured by passenger miles—and have led the industry year after year in customer satisfaction, as measured by the American Customer Satisfaction Index.

Southwest is one of the most frequently cited and intensely studied corporations in the world, for its many innovations and successes. But I believe the greatest innovation that Colleen Barrett and Herb Kelleher pioneered in creating the Southwest phenomenon (if you can call it an *innovation*) was this: they paid close attention to how they made their people *feel*.

I thought about this same idea a year earlier, in the summer of 2009, when I heard a fascinating detail emerge in the story of Laura Ling and Euna Lee, the two American journalists who were held captive in North Korea for five months. The two had been apprehended and arrested while making a documentary about North Korean defectors. Convicted of illegal entry, they were sentenced to twelve years of hard labor. After months of frantic efforts to negotiate with the country's eccentric and notoriously intransigent leader, Kim Jong-il, Americans received word through Laura Ling's sister, Lisa, that the Korean *would* agree to talk with an envoy from the United States—but only if that envoy were former president Bill Clinton.

President Clinton made the trip to North Korea, and on August 4, the two men spent several hours together speaking on a wide range of issues, followed by a reception and dinner in the former US president's honor. The following day the two captives were released.

What was it that broke through the diplomatic stalemate and caused Kim to make this invitation? The answer revealed itself in this fascinating detail: when the two men met, Kim reminded Clinton of a condolence letter the US president had written the North

Korean leader during the 1990s when he was in the Oval Office. "You were the first person," Kim told him, "who reached out to me when my father died—even before my allies. I've always remembered that."

Who would have imagined that such a modest gesture of simple human thoughtfulness would be the impetus for solving a crisis of international diplomacy some fifteen years later?

This is the core insight I have sought to point out throughout this book: that how you treat people, how you make them feel, how you connect with them, and how conscious you stay of that connection, not only determines the kinds of relationships and collaborations you'll have, it is what determines your bottom-line results. Whether it is the profitability of a business, the social impact of a nonprofit, or the extent of learning and growth in the classroom, your productivity is an expression of your leadership and the impact it has on the people you work with. The lesson of Southwest Airlines is the same as the lesson of Brazeway under Stephanie Boyse, Marshalls under Jerry Rossi, Borghese under Georgette Mosbacher, the SBA under Erskine Bowles, the University of Miami under Donna Shalala, or my daughter Madison's first-grade classroom under Kathleen Fucci: if you put *people* at the top of your agenda, you will greatly increase your results.

The truth of life is that it doesn't unfold through lofty mission statements or happen in broad strokes. It is a personal, everyday experience for every one of us.

When I spoke recently with Jerry Rossi, now group president of the TJX Companies, about his leadership philosophy, he said:

"I was thinking about your question, about why it is that people respect one leader but not another, why they are more productive in this environment but not that one. I think it's in your DNA.

You can teach people to do all the analysis, how to be strategic and global and all the other fancy words they have in B school—but what it really comes down to is being a decent human being.

"This is the thing so much of corporate America is completely missing. If you treat people with dignity and respect, if you treat them like human beings, you'll get it back tenfold."

I've been fortunate to find myself working in exceptional circumstances with extraordinary people, from President Clinton to Dick Darman, Donna Shalala and Alexis Herman to Georgette Mosbacher, David Gergen to Warren Bennis and many more. But these experiences and relationships have only served to show me that the qualities I admire in these remarkable men and women are not unique to an elite echelon or rarefied few. As I said in the first pages of the introduction, *leadership is everywhere*. What I saw in the Oval Office I also witnessed in Erica Simons's second-grade classroom. The insights I gleaned in the halls of Harvard I also encountered around the kitchen tables of volunteers throughout the nation in such experiences as the Obama campaign and the Clinton administration's At the Table program.

All these experiences have served to shed light on the same simple truths about leadership:

Becoming an effective leader—someone who is able to rally others around a cause, who inspires others to collaborate towards a common goal, who can bring people together to make a powerfully positive difference in the world—starts with leading ourselves. The bedrock of leadership, it seems to me, is honest self-reflection and a personal commitment to the lifelong pursuit of unblinking self-knowledge.

Being an effective leader often has less to do with knowing the answers, and far more to do with being willing to ask the important questions—and listening to the input, experiences, and perspectives of those around you. The answers are most often right in our midst, just waiting for a leader to recognize, articulate, and act on them.

And finally, good leadership at its core is about the positive feelings it creates.

Often we don't live as consciously as we could. It is so easy to slip into autopilot and forget that the people we meet along our path are human beings with emotions like ourselves. I have been puzzled sometimes by how people in leadership positions, people whose words and actions will have a lasting impact on many others, can be tone deaf to the actual effect their behavior has. What does it take to change that? It simply takes the commitment to live consciously, to make ourselves aware of the people around us, personally and professionally, and how we affect them, for better or for worse. And that makes the simple difference between engagement and disengagement, profit and loss, success and failure.

Imagine a world where people felt valued, appreciated, and understood, both at work and at home. It's a beautiful thought.

AFTERWORD BY WARREN BENNIS

Leadership in Everyday Life

Reading this book brings back memories of hanging out with Betsy in the early years of the new century when we were colleagues, working with David Gergen to establish the Center for Public Leadership at Harvard. Natural storytellers, we would swap tale after tale about our own leadership experiences, each of which seemed exotically fascinating to the other. Exotic and fascinating in part, as I think about it now, because our stories were so different.

For one thing, they were several generations apart: mine, about the Depression and World War II; hers, about serving President Clinton as senior adviser on women's issues and building an insurance and financial services business. Age and gender differences aside, we also grew up in totally different neighborhoods: Betsy, a blond California girl, and her pal Warren, a Jewish kid from the Bronx.

And yet we shared an almost instantaneous affinity.

Through the shining ether of time, it now becomes clear to me that this natural empathy was based on our shared core beliefs about leadership—beliefs to which Betsy, in this book, brilliantly writes the lyrics, in three verses:

219

1. The hardest thing to manage is oneself.
2. The DNA of leadership is relationship-based collaboration. "What is that particular quality certain people have," she asks (and later answers), "that causes those around them to engage fully and feel connected?"
3. Leadership is about bringing out the best in others, as well as in ourselves.

As she describes in her introduction, one of Betsy's daughter's teachers recently asked her what leadership was all about. I love her response: "Successful leaders bring out the most productive feelings in those around them," then adding, "like what you do here with the kids in your class." Which reminded me of Lincoln's rueful appeal in his first inaugural address: "The mystic chords of memory . . . all over this broad land, will yet swell the chorus of the Union, when again touched, as surely they will be, by the better angels of our nature." Well, yes, Lincoln and many others have said it all before, though none approaching Lincoln's aching eloquence. In fact, it's an anthem, an obbligato in the canon of most contemporary leadership books. Throwing to the winds the conceit of modesty, many of us who could be included in that canon have been writing and singing similar lyrics over the past several decades.

Which leads me to ask why this book is unique and well worth a careful reading, or even two.

Perhaps most important is Betsy's unique voice. Imagine Forrest Gump, reincarnated as an intelligent, well-educated woman who travels around the country and somehow finds herself at the elbow of some of the most seminal events of the past two decades. And who, along the way, meets and gets to know, and in some cases even to influence, just about every Page One leader of the time. That's the voice that hums throughout the pages of this book.

The second thing that stands out for me is the quality and resonance of her stories. As I said earlier, she's a natural at it. Natural storytellers know that a good story is one that the audience identifies with—and that a good story stays with you, like a memorable sound bite. Which is why one of my favorite chapters is the one entitled, "Respect: Seeing Past the Sunglasses."

It's about the boss of a large national retail chain, who walks into the elevator of his building one day on the way up to his office. "There was just one other person in the elevator with me, a young woman with her head down. It was the middle of winter, and dark outside—and she was wearing sunglasses." The boss doesn't know her; she is one of 1,400 employees who work in that building. He decides to introduce himself, invites her to have a cup of coffee. He politely suggests she take off her sunglasses. After a bit of gentle prodding, she does—and her two black eyes tell him what she is afraid to put into words. What he sees leads Jerry Rossi, president of Marshalls (now group president of the TJX Companies), to become a founding father and national spokesman for the nonprofit Family Violence Prevention Fund. It changes his life and the lives of countless others.

Betsy ends this story with a profoundly simple line: "Jerry took the time to recognize that there was a *person* behind the sunglasses."

As I said: a memorable sound bite.

One last note that goes back to the story of Betsy's adorable daughter, Madison, and her teacher. It also signals the title of this afterword.

After Betsy tells the teacher what leaders do, the teacher responds, "Oh, I don't really see myself as a leader."

"Are you kidding?" says Betsy. "You're teaching all these children how to read and write, how to share and other important life skills. They are growing and developing their sense of self-worth, and you are right in the middle of that process, teaching them how to learn and nurture their own abilities. You're leading them into their future!"

As you can probably tell, I love this book.

I love it primarily because Betsy's take on leadership is about how we live our lives, about the fact that leadership is integral to our being. She is facing us with a reality, perhaps, at times, an inconvenient reality: that we are all leaders, whether we know it or not, whether we like it or not. She is telling us that leading is not based on a position or even a choice. *How* we lead is our only option.

And we can learn a lot about that by reading this book.

ACKNOWLEDGMENTS

I have to begin by thanking Spencer Johnson, the author of *Who Moved My Cheese?* Spencer is responsible for this book coming together, both through his excitement about the idea of the project and through his willingness to introduce me to his literary agent, Margret McBride. Spencer and I had a spark of connection the moment we first crossed paths because of our mutual interest in leadership. Spencer, I will never be able to fully put into words how grateful I will always be to you for believing in me.

Margret McBride is not only my literary agent but also a unique gift in my life. Her joy is infectious; she is truly one of the happiest people I have the privilege to know. Margret saw the potential of this book and put together the team that made it possible. Margret, you brought pure joy to this project, and your enthusiasm kept us all going through the many hurdles a book project can face.

Margret introduced me to John David Mann, my cowriter. John and I began this project as colleagues and, as we charted our way through the process of learning how to work together and finding this book's shape, also became good friends. He helped me unpeel the onion of the leadership stories in this book and listened to hours of recounted experiences from my life, some relevant to the book and some not. John, you are truly a gifted writer, and this book owes a debt to the insights and skills you brought to the table.

Thank you to Judith Curr, the publisher of Atria Books, for believing in this project, and to our editor, Peter Borland, for his inspiring leadership. Judith, I have felt incredibly supported by you and the rest of the stellar team at Atria at every step and will be forever grateful to you. You exemplify leadership with beauty and grace. Peter, your boundless energy and tireless enthusiasm for this project, along with your amazing skill at putting your finger on what it was we were trying to say and finding just the right words, has never ceased to amaze me. You challenged me to go beyond what I thought was possible; I consider you my friend for life.

My thanks go to my parents, Judy and Steve Myers, who spent hours listening to my ideas and were always willing to read the latest version and make suggestions in the text. Mom and Dad, you have always been my biggest champions; your love has been a warm blanket of support throughout my life. My thanks also go to my sisters, Dee Dee Myers and JoJo Proud, for their wisdom and support. The two of you are my confidantes, and our shared history and friendship have been an anchor in my life.

Thanks to my many women friends, who share a special place in my life and whose perspectives and support keep me going. A special thanks to those who took the time to read portions of this book (in some cases, *all* of it), including Sava Berhané, Louisa Bohm, Susan Clampitt, Judy Gold, Hattie Hill, Pat McGinnis, Diane Rosenfeld, Roberta Oster Sachs, Maris Segal, Pnina Stisser, Ali Webb, and Madelyn Yucht. A special thanks to Amy Millman, who went beyond the call of friendship on this project and who is truly one of my most important mentors.

Thank you to the Keller women, Ann, Suzy, and Kim, for your support and friendship over the years.

Thanks to Sandy Miller and Andrés Tapia, who spent hours

with me at Hewitt exploring the material of this book for a leadership training program; to Toddie Downs, for her editing input, and Linda Clemons, for her enthusiasm, support, and marketing genius; and to Sam Horn, who is responsible for helping me gain clarity around the idea of *leadership as feelings.* I also want to thank Junius Podrug and Helen Rees, who inspired in me the confidence to write this book.

To all the leadership experts, too many to name, who have touched my life and taught me so much, and especially to Warren Bennis, Ken Blanchard, David Gergen, and Elliott Masie. Your ideas and input helped this book become what it is, and your friendship is an inspiration.

To the many people who graciously gave their time to be interviewed for this book, including Barbara Annis, Barbara Barry, Judy Biggs, Erskine Bowles, Stephanie Hickman Boyse, Frank Brosens, Elizabeth Bryant, Bonnie Campbell, Roxanne Cason, Ruth Cox, Joyce Curll, Myrto Flessas, Marshall Ganz, Deborah Gist, Kathleen Manning Hall, Alexis Herman, Paul Hodes, Barbara Kellerman, Mary Frances Kelley, Tanisha Kirkland, Annie McLane Kuster, Robin Leeds, Georgette Mosbacher, Janet Petersen, Anne Reed, Jerry Rossi, Victoria Salinas, Laureen Seeger, Donna Shalala, Sally Smith, Ann Stock, Kelly Taylor, Elizabeth Vale, and Lezlee Westine. Some of your stories are included here and some, owing to the rigors of editing and page space, are not; my thanks to all of you for your time and generosity.

I want to thank Rob Keller, who walked the journey of this book with me, spending endless hours talking about these stories and being my sounding board for ideas about leadership. When I had writer's block you sat with me, challenging me to write down everything that came into my head. Your insights have always broadened my perspective and given me new ways to think about things. I will always be grateful to you. And my special thanks go to our daughter, Madison, for a wisdom and fresh perspective on the world that constantly amazes me. Madison, you are truly a gift in my life.

Finally, to all the readers and kindred spirits who read these pages and join me in exploring the path of leadership: my thanks to each and every one of you.

Index

227

19, 129–30; goals and, 117, 1129; how to take the lead and, 129–31; listening and, 125–27; in marriage, 123–24; morale and, 114; Obama presidential campaign and, 105–8; Olympic torch relay and, 101–5; outbox strategy and, 115–19, 130; priorities and, 112–14, 116, 129–30; questions and, 125–27, 131; relationships and, 122–24; SBA transformation and, 109–15, 125–26; welfare reform and, 112–14; on why, 127–29

Clinton, Bill: approval rating for, 66–67; connection and, 46–47, 66; domestic violence issues and, 71, 74–75; Gergen and, 90; Kim Jong-il and, 215–16; leadership style of, 47; legacy of, 112, 113; as listener, 76–77, 171–73; as loving job, 20; Myers admiration for, 217; Myers decision to join Obama campaign and, 91; 1996 reelection campaign of, 23; SBA and, 109, 110, 111, 112, 113, 115, 127–29; telling the truth to, 171–73; welfare reform and, 76–79

Clinton, Hillary: as connecting with others, 46–47; Myers decision to join Obama campaign and, 88–92; presidential campaign

of, 88–99, 187, 195, 196, 202; supporters of, 87–99; women entrepreneurs and, 110

Clinton White House: domestic violence issues and, 71–72; Myers observations about leadership at, 3; Myers reflections about her experiences in, 30–31; senior staff meetings at, 82–83. *See also* Small Business Administration; Women's Office; *specific person or issue*

collaboration: action and, 137–38, 161; in bad times, 138, 139–40, 161; Bennis views about, 220; clarity and, 136; common ground and, 147–49; communication and, 138, 139–42, 161; connection and, 48–49, 153, 154; continuity and, 134–36; as core idea of leadership, 15–16, 133–62, 216, 220; differing points of view and, 152–60, 161, 162; difficult relationships and, 145–47, 149–52, 161–62; effectiveness and, 133, 137–38, 145, 150, 161; feelings and, 140; how to take the lead and, 161–62; lack of, 142–45; learning and, 152–57; listening and, 137, 138, 161; new kind of leadership and, 10; openness and, 133–34; respect and, 138, 139–40, 153,

people: as mattering, 16, 74, 99, 216
personal advisory board, 173–75, 189
Personal Responsibility
      Reconciliation and Work
      Opportunity Act. *See* welfare
      reform
Peters, Tom, 10, 104
Petersen, Brian, 53, 54
Petersen, Janet, 52–54, 55–56
Plouffe, David, 106, 107, 114
political appointees, 64–67
Porter, Roger, 156
Prine, Reenie, 212
priorities: clarity and, 112–14, 116,
      129–30; shift from Clinton
      to Bush White House and,
      135, 136
Proud, Mary Jo (Jo Jo),2, 36, 65
Public Liaison Office (White
      House), 78–79
Purdum, Kate, 178–79
Purdum, Todd, 178

Q
questions: authenticity and, 29, 33;
      clarity and, 108, 113–14, 125–
      27, 129, 131; collaboration
      and, 136, 149–50; connecting
      and, 51–52, 66, 69, 131; about
      engagement, 15; focusing,
      129; about handling difficult
      relationships, 149–50;
      importance of asking, 51–52,
      125–27, 131, 217–18; leaders'
      willingness to ask, 11, 12–13,
      125–27, 131, 217–18; learning

and, 173, 183; about mentors,
      183; and Myers curiosity
      about leadership, 3; new kind
      of leadership and, 11, 12–13;
      personal advisory board and,
      173; about what is leadership,
      2–3

R
race: Obama speech about, 203–5
Rachael (Madison's friend), 17, 193,
      194
Reed, Anne, 67–68
relationships: authenticity and, 38;
      benefits of good, 50; building,
      49–52, 68–69; clarity and,
      122–24; difficult, 145–47,
      149–52, 161–62; knowing
      your own story and, 24–25;
      leaving, 152, 162; living
      with difficult, 151, 152, 162;
      maintaining past, 89–92, 100;
      new era of leadership and, 9;
      during Obama presidential
      campaign, 150–51; personal
      advisory board and, 173–75;
      repairing/fixing, 150, 152,
      161; sharing and, 50, 150,
      161; technology and, 60–
      62; women as leaders and,
      8. *See also* collaboration;
      connection; mentors
respect: being tuned out and,
      82–84, 100; collaboration
      and, 138, 139–40, 153, 154;
      communication and, 84–